WHERE STANDS DEMOCRACY?

WHERE STANDS DEMOCRACY

DEMOCRACY

?

A Collection of Essays by Members of the
FABIAN SOCIETY

HAROLD J. LASKI
HAMILTON FYFE
LEONARD BARNES
R. H. S. CROSSMAN
G. D. H. COLE
K. ZILLIACUS

Essay Index Reprint Series

BOOKS FOR LIBRARIES PRESS
FREEPORT, NEW YORK

First Published 1940
Reprinted 1970

STANDARD BOOK NUMBER:
8369-1651-4

LIBRARY OF CONGRESS CATALOG CARD NUMBER:
76-117788

PRINTED IN THE UNITED STATES OF AMERICA

64346

CONTENTS

vii

1

GOVERNMENT IN WARTIME

HAROLD J. LASKI

GOVERNMENT IN WARTIME

1 DEMOCRACY AND WAR

GOVERNMENT in wartime may be described as aiming at a twofold objective. It seeks, on the one hand, to break the will of the enemy by concentrating against him the maximum resources, spiritual and material, that are at the disposal of the nation; and it seeks, in the second place, so to deal with him when victory has been won, that the conditions of a durable peace are laid.

Certain preliminary essentials clearly emerge from this objective. It is necessary that the nation should be at unity with itself; and the greater the degree in which this unity is the product of consent, the greater is the spiritual energy of which a government is able to dispose. A sullen unity, a unity, even more, that has to be imposed by coercion, is not one that is likely to survive the stress and strain to which a nation is subjected by war. There is an important advantage, therefore, to any government which wages it when the sense is widespread that the circumstances of its origin provided no alternative to conflict. But hardly less important is the ability of statesmen to persuade the nation that the methods by which they conduct the war, and the ends they seek to attain by victory. are such as to commend themselves to reasonable men and women who are free to think for themselves. There is a life-giving power in that ability for which

3

no other quality, when the strength of the combatants is approximately equal, can ever be a compensation.

It is the central problem of the British Government to adjust itself to this perspective. To do so means a basic reliance upon the traditional framework of our institutions. Deviation from them must not contradict their inner and essential principles if it is to maintain their moral energy unimpaired. For we know those principles as a man knows a suit that has grown to his shape. We are at ease with them. We have the elbow room from their operation that gives our citizenship a positive character, which makes us more than plastic material to be shaped by the Government into whatever mould it pleases. A Government in Great Britain cannot wage war successfully if it seeks to destroy values to which the mass of the nation has pinned its faith. Those values are summarised for us in the system of parliamentary democracy; we could not win the war at the price of its destruction. A Government which sought to do so would at once destroy the unity of the nation. Thereby its own will to victory would be impaired. It would face an internal dissension so profound that it could not hope effectively to mobilise its material resources upon a scale adequate to victory against a powerful opponent. It would bring itself certainly, and the nation at least possibly, to disaster.

It therefore follows that, for us in Great Britain, the structural problems of government in wartime (with which alone I am here concerned) are adjustments of the classical technique of Parliamentary government and not its abandonment. They must be built round the view that, whether for peace or war, our institutions are, in a general way, methodologically adequate. What we need is to quicken and to unify their operation for the objectives I have already defined. I do not need to discuss the issue of the inherent ability of a Parliamentary democracy to win a great war. Not only was that ability established by the experience of the war of 1914; it is also notable, as has often been pointed out, that the stablest societies in the modern era are those in which the tradition of parliamentary democracy is most deeply rooted. That stability, indeed, is one of the vital sources of their strength. It has bred in their citizens a power to resist violent change, an ability freely to make the compromises which social life requires, which is unequalled in any other form of institution.

But the necessity of adapting parliamentary democracy to the demands of war is a matter of common agreement. Parliamentary government is, normally, leisurely government; war calls for rapidity of decision. Parliamentary government is, normally again, built upon the assumption of an Opposition that seeks to destroy the general credit of the Ministry in office by obstructing its measures in detail; war calls for an Opposition that opposes only on the large grounds of vital principle since, otherwise, there is no national unity behind the direction of the Government's power. Certain other issues call for examination, even if, when examined, they do not necessarily call for revaluation. There is the problem of the place of the expert in a parliamentary democracy at war; is it lesser or greater than in the times of peace? There is the problem of local government; how far, granted the imperative need of a unified

use of our resources, can we allow free play to elected
and decentralised initiative? There is the problem,
further—on every count a grave one—of civil liberties in
wartime. Are there more narrow limits to their operation
in matters like freedom of speech and of association? If
so, what are those limits? If not, what are the grounds
upon which the maintenance of normal procedure can be
maintained? These are the main matters to which I
shall draw your attention. But, as you will see, there is
inherent in my discussion of them a conclusion of great
import upon which it is desirable to say something now.

'War,' said Edmund Burke, 'never leaves where it
found a nation.' On any showing, especially nowadays,
it is the profoundest experience through which a
nation can pass. It disturbs every wonted routine.
It forces upon us innovation and experiment in every
department of social life. Above all, war is organisation, and, at least while it lasts, it suspends every
item in the formulae of *laissez-faire*. It is a dynamic
experience; and it becomes essential to find the proper
dynamic for a democracy in war. The innovations and
experiments create new, and vast, expectations; the
success of a democracy depends upon its power to
answer those expectations. Unless its Government
can do this, both in the ends it seeks, and in the
methods by which it attains those ends, it will not continue to possess the confidence of citizens; and, in a
parliamentary democracy, a Government which cannot
command that confidence cannot successfully wage a
war. As a Government, therefore, it has not merely
to show a will to win, not merely, even, a power to
win; it has to show also what are its will and power

to win for. The discovery of this, in such fashion as to command the profound approval of the masses, is what I have called the dynamic of democracy. Only a Government capable of this discovery is likely to win the war and retain its democratic form. Without that capacity, it deprives itself of its popular foundation. It has then to rely upon a technique of coercion which, by its very nature, alters the foundations of the state.

2 THE CABINET

It is universally agreed that the peace time form of Cabinet is unsuited to the requirements of war. It is too big for despatch, for secrecy, for a tightly-knit unity of mind. The problem then becomes one of deciding, first, the kind of size a War Cabinet should have, and, second, the relation of its members to the process of administration.

This is clearly an issue upon which it is too early to speak with any confidence and that for two reasons. The only alternative historic model to that of Mr. Chamberlain's system is the War Cabinet of Mr Lloyd George; and it is not easy to say whether the differences between them will be found to lie in structural principle, or in the very different person- alities of the men who composed them. Mr. Lloyd George's principle had, at any rate, the great merit of clarity. He assumed that the War Cabinet must be small; after the addition of General Smuts, it consisted of six men. He assumed that its members must be able to give their whole time to the general principles involved in directing, in its fullest sense, the strategy of the war. He therefore separated policy from

administration; only one of its members, Mr. Bonar
Law, was, as Chancellor of the Exchequer, charged
with the control of a great department. The others
were left wholly free to make general policy, and its
detailed application was left to discussion between
the War Cabinet, or one of more of its members, and
the heads of the Ministries, whether politicians or civil
servants, concerned with its decisions. He believed,
thirdly, that the function of supreme coordination was
the central business of the Prime Minister. He did not
think that task compatible with continuous attention
to the House of Commons. The leadership of the House
was, therefore, entrusted by him to Mr Bonar Law;
he himself only attended the House on exceptional
occasions when the matter for debate seemed of such
outstanding importance that only the Prime Minister
could handle it in a decisively authoritative way.

Mr. Chamberlain has proceeded upon a different
basis altogether. He has, indeed, drastically reduced
the size of the Cabinet; it now consists of nine, instead
of twenty-three members. Five of its members,[1]
three of them the heads of the Service Departments,
have heavy administrative duties; four others, including
the Prime Minister himself, are virtually Ministers
without portfolio. It is understood that Sir Samuel
Hoare, as Lord Privy Seal, presides over a committee
of Ministers not in the War Cabinet, who are responsible
for home affairs; and the economic coordination of
war effort is entrusted to the Chancellor of the
Exchequer, who has the part-time services of Lord

[1] Mr. Eden, as Secretary of the Dominions, attends the meetings
of the War Cabinet, but is not technically a member of it.

Stamp, with a small staff, as his adviser. The Prime Minister retains the leadership of the House of Commons, where he is in constant attendance. He not only makes his weekly statement on the war, which is usually followed by a brief debate. He also answers questions; and in all major matters of foreign policy, the presence of the Foreign Secretary in the House of Lords means that the major burden of handling these issues necessarily falls also upon him.

What is to be said about these two very different conceptions? The Lloyd George scheme was, I think, based upon a fundamental fallacy—that it is possible to separate policy from administration. 'He who has in his hands the execution of measures,' said Sir Henry Taylor, 'is in truth the very master of them.' There is evidence and to spare that the Lloyd George system worked far less smoothly than its eminent author would wish us to imagine. Much of its time was spent on arguing out its decisions with departments. Still more was devoted to settling differences between them. The absence from its deliberations of the Ministers concerned with the application of policy meant a good deal of incoherence. There was a time when one foreign policy was being conducted by the Prime Minister and another foreign policy by the Foreign Secretary. There was inadequate continuity of contact between the War Cabinet and departmental ministers, on the one hand, and between the former and the responsible civil servants on the other. There was always doubt whether the War Cabinet itself was fully acquainted with the mind of the departments themselves; and it was never easy,

B

without something akin to an elaborate system of espion-
age, for the Prime Minister to acquaint himself with that
mind.   That the inner relationships were unhappy is
proved, I think, by the experience of the War Office—
witness the Maurice debate—on the one hand, and that
of the Admiralty—witness the account of Lord Jellicoe
—on the other. No doubt Mr. Lloyd George's brilliant and
remarkable energy triumphed over these, and similar
difficulties. But that does not prove that the system was
inherently right; it proves only that a remarkable Prime
Minister can transcend the weaknesses of his own system.

For the truth is that the principles of administration
cannot be separated from the practice of administration.
The men who make the decisions must be those through
whose hands the pivotal papers pass. They do the
work of selection out of which principles emerge;
and the work of selection is itself the necessary ground-
work upon which alone right decisions can be taken.
That is why, to take an obvious instance, there is
always a special relation between the Prime Minister
and the Foreign Secretary; unless the contact between
them was close and unremitting, the ability of the
former to keep his hands upon the main outlines
of foreign policy would be non-existent. If this
separation grows, departments begin to live a life
of their own; and the War Cabinet becomes, not a maker
of policy, but a corrector of mistakes. That this is the
case has already been shown in the case of the Ministry
of Information. It is not merely that the Ministry started
on a bad foundation. Even more, it is the fact that a
Minister in Sir John Reith's position has either got
to go his own way, independently of the War

Cabinet, or he has continuously to consult it on every important question which arises, and if public opinion is dissatisfied with the Ministry, if the stream of criticism is perpetual, the War Cabinet has, in fact, continually to acquaint itself with details, evaluate them, evolve them into principles, while it is all the time protesting that only freedom from the consideration of details will enable it properly to fulfil its function of laying down the large outlines of policy for the conduct of the war.

I believe, therefore, that the central idea of Mr Chamberlain's War Cabinet is better than that of Mr Lloyd George. But I think that Mr Chamberlain's principle suffers, in its present form, from serious errors of structure upon which too much emphasis can hardly be laid. There are four Service Ministers out of nine, all upon an equal footing; there is already material here for inter-departmental friction. The economic front and the home service front are quite inadequately represented by the Chancellor of the Exchequer—the quintessence of that Treasury mind which excludes from the area of desirable action all expenditure upon innovations—and a Minister without portfolio who has no direct control over the spending departments outside those of defence. There is something to be said for Ministers without portfolio when they have the special experience that has fallen over so many years to Lord Hankey's lot; especially if they can relieve the Prime Minister from his inescapable burden, or tackle inter-departmental questions with the acute special expertise that experience must have given.

But a War Cabinet, I suggest, must coordinate in the context of direct control over the departments.

Ministers must be in and with them, not aloof and beyond. If this is right, the structure of the War Cabinet begins to define itself in a different way from that of Mr Chamberlain. The Prime Minister is the Keystone of the Arch; as Lord Oxford saw, at the time of his conflict with Mr Lloyd George, he must be in charge of the team in its daily work, or, effectively, he really ceases to be Prime Minister. The Chancellor of the Exchequer and the Foreign Secretary must be there; the first is essential for the all-round view of financial policy, as the watch-dog in adapting the financial resources of the country to demanded ends, and the second because no one else can adequately contribute the background of detail which enables the right decisions to be taken in international affairs. These three Ministers are the central focus about which the rest of the structure must be built. Without them, not only is essential information lacking at any given point; still more important, essential continuity of information is lacking which forms the background of wise decision.

But I cannot believe that we need three Service Ministers plus a Minister for the Coordination of Defence. Broadly, he can coordinate if they are his subordinates; he cannot coordinate if they are his equals. In the latter situation, he cannot be more, at best, than a wise man offering the best advice he can, and taking his chance that the quality of his argument will make it prevail. That, clearly, is not coordination in any meaning sense of the term. It is, I think, clear that the present structure overweighs Service representation. Three of the Ministries are in charge of immense departments, swollen out of all proportion to their normal size. They cannot see the interpenetration of their problems from an eminence. The right thing, surely, is to make the Minister for the Coordination of Defence a Minister of Defence in the full sense of the term. He should represent the three Services in the Cabinet. He should have the power to control and coordinate their activities. He would, in that position, not only be able to deal with inter-departmental friction; he would be able, also, and with full knowledge, to see to it that only the vital questions of defence came for decision to the War Cabinet as a whole. I will not deal here with the general argument for a Minister with such powers. I will only say that every case, even that of Lord Haldane, which has been made against it, has been based on arguments of a political, and not of an administrative, nature. These are now irrelevant; and the case for the unity of defence, its unified representation, therefore, in the Cabinet, has become unanswerable if we mean the coordination of the three services to be real.

But, if this be true, the argument applies with even greater force to production for the nourishment of defence. We have now four Ministries concerned with these problems in the major sphere; and four other departments—Transport, Mining, Shipping and Economic Warfare, are integrally related to their work. They are represented in the War Cabinet by the Chancellor of the Exchequer, a Minister who already carries an immense burden, and whose angle of approach is altogether different, even alien, from that of the departments involved. Is it not clear that what we require is a Minister of Economic Coordination, who shall act as the effective head of these seven departments and speak to the issues they raise both in the War Cabinet and in Parliament? He would, this is to say, drive a coherent stream of tendency through their inter-related affairs. He would have the advantage of con-tinuous and detailed contact with them. Their officials would be, in the last resort, directly under his control. He could see that only the largest problems created by their activities come before the War Cabinet; all the minor departmental issues which now arise he would have authority to dispose of himself. Above all, he would speak of those issues with an authority equal to that of the Chancellor of the Exchequer, so that he could confront the Treasury on equal terms. And because he was directly and responsibly related to their adminis-trative process, there would not be the abyss which now yawns between the War Cabinet and economic produc-tion. On this scheme, I believe, some of the major mistakes we have already made, those of the Ministry of Supply, for instance, or of the Ministry of Mines, could have been avoided. Coordination is one thing when it is attempted by a Minister immersed in the facts of his problem; it is a different and, I think, an unsatisfactory thing, when it is attempted by a War Cabinet through a Minister who, like the Chancellor of the Exchequer, is bound to see the whole issue through lenses very different from those which the departments concerned are necessarily using.

Then there is the home service front, health, educa-tion, civil defence, the service of information and propaganda; these, to take the obvious instances, must go on. At present, they are linked to the War

Cabinet through the Lord Privy Seal. But in relation to them, the nature of his office makes him an omnipresence brooding in the sky above them, rather than one with them and of them. His officials are not theirs. He does not see their problems at first-hand. He deals only with the matters they feel they must bring before the War Cabinet, or those which outside opinion forces upon its attention. Here, again, there is no adequate coordination; and it will have been noticed that whenever objection to any decision is taken powerful enough to compel attention, it is driven to the Prime Minister for decision. The Labour Party is dissatisfied with the Ministry of Information; it goes to the Prime Minister. The Trades Union Congress is dissatisfied with the Ministry of Supply; it goes to the Prime Minister. He becomes the conduit-pipe through which all major decisions must go; and he cannot have the time to do more than lay down, in a superficial way, lines of policy that other Ministers must carry out in detail, and that where the detail is the essence of the lines of policy in their living reality.

It seems to me, therefore, that we require in the War Cabinet a Minister for the Coordination of Home Services who will act as the controlling force in their disposition. He will have to see that they are maintained in the fullest vigour that the demands of the war make possible; and he must represent their problems with fitting urgency in the War Cabinet. Are we, for instance, to continue the system of half-education that has now come into being? Are we to develop a policy for evacuees which will give some stability to the situation in which they find themselves?

Does the War Cabinet adequately grasp the problems that have been raised by pensions and war allowances? I need not multiply instances. What is painfully clear at present is the absence of structural mechanisms permitting their proper consideration upon a unified plane.

On this scheme, there are two ranges of problems, both of them vital, for which I have made no allowance. There is the problem of India; and there are the problems connected with the Dominions, the colonies and the dependencies. Before the war is over, they will clearly have to be considered at their foundation; some of them, India, for example, and Palestine, may make the difference between life and death for a Government, according to whether a wise decision is taken, since their repercussions are world-wide. My own view is that the general oversight of them, for the war period, should be in the hands of the Secretary for the Dominions. He already attends the War Cabinet; Indian and colonial questions are clearly and properly relevant to his interests. If he were given the task of coordinating work now divided between three departments, there would, I suggest, be a saving of time and a gain in coherency.

What results from this survey? On this structural pattern, we should have a War Cabinet of eight, two of whom, the Prime Minister, and one Minister without portfolio, would have no departmental functions. The Foreign Secretary, and the Chancellor of the Exchequer, have already, in their own departments, a full administrative burden. Each of the remainder would be in charge of a related group of departments, the general problems of which he would control up to that point where they were of sufficient importance to demand Cabinet discussion. The internal policy of his group would be worked out by him in conjunction with his colleagues; and he would be directly in a position not only to maintain a general oversight, but also, where he deemed it desirable, to enquire into particular detail. He could prevent the separation of departmental traditions from leading to those internal conflicts of which the record of the last war is so full. He could save the War Cabinet and the Prime Minister from the consideration of many problems, above all those of external pressure and internecine dispute, which now burden them heavily. This structure implies a Cabinet of eight members, effectively two less than at present, and it covers by direct contact the whole field of administration, internal and external. It is, therefore, large enough to prevent the separation of policy from administration which was, I have argued, the main flaw in the Lloyd George scheme; and it is small enough, if its members are wisely chosen, to put the Prime Minister in command of a genuinely unified scheme. It is, finally, a pattern into which it is possible to fit any new departments the need for which may arise during the war; for it has coherence at the top of its pyramid, and a sufficient flexibility at the base to enable them to be dovetailed logically into the general structure it implies. It is administration by the grouping of related functions into a coherency unified by similarity of purpose. That, I suggest, is the proper way to seize the War Cabinet of those large issues decisions upon which ought alone to be its fundamental preoccupation.

3 PARLIAMENT

War, under modern conditions, means the conference of immense powers and wide discretion upon the Executive; and safeguards against their abuse are of the essence of democratic life. That is not all. It may be necessary not only to criticise, even to attack, what may be termed the internal direction of the war; it may be necessary also to criticise the general purposes the Government has in view. There may be dissent about the ultimate objectives; there may be disagreement about the timing of a peace-offer; there may be doubt about the general energy of the Government, or the quality of its personnel. Unless we assume—as in a political democracy we cannot assume—that the function of the citizen in wartime is that of silent obedience only, it follows that Parliament must assume a central place in the life of the nation.

For it is there, above all, that grievances may be expressed, demands made, criticism formulated. It is there, also, that Ministers can be held effectively responsible for what they have done. A Parliament that is vigilant in its scrutiny of Government action, in which members are attentive to popular experience, in which Ministers are made to take account of its meaning, can perform a service of inestimable value. Nowhere in the world is there a Government good enough to be above the right to be examined about its policy; and the greater the powers it exercises, the greater, proportionately, is the importance of that examination.

From this I draw two inferences. I believe, first, that the more fully the normal functions of Parliament are maintained, the more efficient is likely to be the conduct of the war by those who are charged with it. I believe, secondly, that the power to change the Government by the normal constitutional procedure is essential to the preservation of political democracy.

For all government, at best, is a fallible thing; and to compel it to reasoned defence for its actions is to compel it to act with some measure, at least, of reasonableness. No doubt, it is entitled, in wartime, to freedom from merely obstructive attack. But if we agree that it is its business to be able to justify what it proposes to do, then it follows logically that it must be able to defend its proposals against whatever case the critics can make against them. Once it is freed from that necessity, it becomes a dictatorship; and the evidence is I think overwhelming that the citizens of this country are not prepared to entrust dictatorial powers to any body of men. They take the view, in my judgment the one view that history supports, that in any community those who exercise dictatorial powers are bound, in the long run, to abuse them.

I think, therefore, that the Labour Party was fundamentally right in its refusal to enter Mr Chamberlain's Government. It may share with that Government the common view that the war must be won; but there is certainly wide divergence between the Labour Party and Mr Chamberlain about the methods by which victory is to be obtained, and it may well prove, as the months go by, that there is wide divergence also about the ends for which victory is to be attained. It is better that there should be a responsible body of men in Parliament, able, should dissatisfaction arise, to represent that dissatisfaction in a coherent way, able, also, if need be, to drive the Government from office, than that the process of criticism should be destroyed by the formation of those peculiar and complicated loyalties that are inherent in any all-party coalition.

Nor is this all. The very fact that a genuine Opposition is in being has two important effects. It is a focus from which lines of connection radiate to those who believe themselves to be unjustly affected by Government decisions. It enables criticism to be more than a formality. It compels ministers not merely to seem to give satisfaction, but actually to strive to give it. It compels discussion; and unless there is discussion in a democracy, it has no chance of survival. Even in the brief period that has passed since the outbreak of war, the importance of the Opposition's existence has been clear. On the problems connected with evacuation; on the Ministry of Information; on the safeguards of public liberty; on the problem of India; on the issues connected with the Ministry of Supply; the critical examination of Government decisions by the House of Commons has already proved of extraordinary value. Without it, grave mistakes would have been made, serious inefficiencies would have been concealed, that are prevented, or repaired, because Ministers know not only that they must answer for what they have done, but, even more, that their future as Ministers depends upon their ability to satisfy the House that the tasks with which they are charged are performed with adequacy.

I go even further. I think it is vital to keep alive the party structure of the House in the kind of emergency we confront. It is not merely, as Bagehot said, that party government is the vital principle of representative government. It is also that the philosophic abyss on important points of doctrine which separates the Government from the Opposition would not be bridged by a weak compromise in which each sacrificed its vital principles for a superficial unity. It is far better, above all in wartime, that responsibility for policy should be built upon principles that are clearly understood and tested in action by their results, than that it should be built upon an attempt to sacrifice principle and thus evade responsibility by makeshift adjustments in which each party agrees to surrender clarity in decision in order to maintain a formal union. This would necessarily result not merely in a policy of half-measures; it would mean that everyone agreed not to speak his full mind, above all when it was vital that the full mind should be spoken. It would mean that the ventilation of grievance and the expression of dissent were stifled at every serious point lest they make it difficult for parties to live in harmony in the same Cabinet. That would mean not only weak government; it would mean, also, a continuous underground pressure upon members of the House not to raise inconvenient questions. Yet, in wartime, it is almost always the inconvenient questions that need to be raised. You do not answer them, as an all-party Government is tempted invariably to do, by the dishonest pretence that they do not exist.

It is worth pointing out, further, two things. Because Parliament is real (which is another way of saying that the Opposition is real) public opinion in the country is kept alive and active. Citizens recognise that they have an organ through which their emotions and ideas, big and small, can be so expressed that they have the chance to make their way effectively to the centre of power. I believe that an active citizenship of this kind is of an importance beyond estimation. It keeps alive the public conscience. It prevents the Government reducing citizens to the status of inert subjects of its own purpose. And the fact that citizens are active has the further immense advantage that it keeps members of Parliament active also. War is too vast an enterprise to permit the classic rigidities of party loyalty to remain untouched. It drives to new thought because it raises problems so new and so profound. There has been, I think, something like a renovation of Parliament in the weeks since the 3rd of September. The very vastness of the powers Ministers have demanded has driven ordinary members not merely to ask whether they ought to be conferred, but, also, whether the men who seek them are the men who ought to exercise them. The Government, no doubt, is a team with the classic collective responsibility; but there is a far less willingness than in normal times to be tender to the inefficient and to the blunderer than in time of peace. There is more independence, more sense that the men chosen to rule must prove themselves by perform-ance, and not obscure their errors behind the screen of party claim, than I can remember in many years. Even a Prime Minister, in this atmosphere, will only survive by his power to win the confidence of a newly critical House by convincing it of something more than good

intentions—I do not think it unlikely prophecy to pre-
dict that this House, even with a vast majority of Tory
members, will be more exacting in its demands upon
Ministers than it has been at any time since 1914.

The results of this will, I venture to assert, penetrate
far into the recesses of the state. There is an important
reciprocity of influence in an active House of Commons
that is a fundamental element in the morale of the
nation. An alert House means an alert public opinion
outside; and this, in its turn, strengthens the alertness
of the House. But the alertness of the House has a
similar repercussion upon the public; and both combine
to influence by their activism the whole process of
administration. This it is which renders Parliament
so vital in wartime. No other institution could take
its place. Our business, indeed, is above all to resolve
with all our power that no other institution shall take
its place. For so long as it maintains its present temper
and its present position, I do not think we need fear
in this country for the future of democratic government.

4   AN ECONOMIC GENERAL STAFF

The problems of the civil service in wartime are
so manifold that I cannot even pretend to touch
upon more than one of them here. Ministries have to
be rapidly improvised; personnel has to be selected
without regard to the standards of admission which
prevail in a period of peace; the technical aspects of
production for war raise issues about the relation
between the expert and the politician of the highest
delicacy. Out of the mass of issues which need analysis,
there is one, above all, to which I want to direct your

attention. I believe it is one upon which there is, perhaps, more confused thinking than upon any other, not least in the Labour Party. If we can get our minds straight upon this, I believe we can enormously clarify the central aspects of wartime administration.

The one to which I refer is the demand for an Economic General Staff. The vital officials of the state, we are told, are so immersed in the details of their departments that they have no time for that coordinated and general planning that is essential to success. Exactly as an army has a general staff to lay down the larger aspects of its policy, so we ought to have a general staff which should coordinate the large outlines of policy within which the different departments concerned with economic planning should function. Its members should be free from departmental duties; they should have the function of taking, not the day-to-day decisions, but the long term views; and they should be able to secure attention for their views from the cabinet—Sir William Beveridge's word is 'compel.'

Now I think that the analogy between the general staff of an army and the proposed Economic General Staff is a wholly false one. The former, within the range of policy to which it is confined, has a pretty specific function; and each of its members, within that range, has, as it were, a function within a function for which he must assume responsibility. That is not the idea of an Economic General Staff in the minds of its sponsors. They are concerned with the whole range of economic policy—finance, commerce, industry, agriculture, labour. They are to develop a unified policy for all these in their majestic interpenetration. They are to shape the direction in which at least seven different ministries now directly participate, in which, also, the contracts departments of at least four other ministries are vitally interested. They are not to be of and in those departments, but above and beyond them. They plan measures in a general way; they do not themselves direct their execution. None of the members of this General Staff can hope to be experts in the detailed policies of all these departments. They are to be expert in coordinating policies developed by experts into unity.

Two criticisms at once occur. Is it not clear, first, that such an Economic General Staff could only be, at best, an intermediate body, presumably of wise men, advising the War Cabinet? They could not plunge into the details of all departmental work— if they did, by definition, they would not have the time to concern themselves with taking large general views valid for a considerable period of time. But if this is the case, are they not at once in two difficulties from neither of which is there any effective escape? (a) Are they not in the difficulty that either they themselves must choose the issues about which they are to coordinate and plan, in which case there is, on all experience, certainty of immense and continuous friction with the departments actually concerned with the execution of measures; or (b) they deal with those larger issues only which the departments choose to submit to them for advice. If the first principle is to be their basis, every difference between the Economic General Staff and a department will become a Cabinet question between that staff and the Minister of the department concerned. If the principle of its functioning

c

is to be the second, because it is then only selectively
relevant to the range of economic policy, it cannot
possibly fulfil the function of planning and coordination.
The first principle means an enormous addition to the
burden of the War Cabinet, as anyone will testify who
knows the ingenuity and persistence of a department in
maintaining ground it has chosen to occupy. The
second abandons altogether the conception of an
Economic General Staff in the sense in which its advocates defend it. On this principle, it is simply a body of
advisers upon problems of an economic character that
may be referred to it; and there is no *a priori* ground
for assuming that its discussion of these will have any
more validity than those of the Cabinet itself, save inso-
far as its members understand them better, and are wiser
about them, than the Prime Minister and his colleagues.

But there is a further difficulty to which I must
refer. Is the Economic General Staff to be built upon
a hierarchical basis, or is it a small committee of
equals? If it is the first, it will clearly make a great
difference whether its head is, say, Mr Keynes or
his eminent antagonist Professor Pigou. And if it is
a small committee of equals, there are few questions
of fundamental importance upon which there is not
at least the inherent probability of a series of reports
between which the War Cabinet will have to choose.
You have only to remember the grave differences
between the defence experts on the Dardanelles
expedition in the last war to realise that the politician,
on all major matters, rarely has a single solution to
approve or reject; he chooses between a number of
conflicting views urged on him with all the ability

and persistence which expertise can command, and the politicians' judgment is not seldom a valuation dependent upon that 'intuition more subtle than any articulate major premiss' of which Mr. Justice Holmes has spoken so wisely. More: many of the problems have a political background upon which the judgment of an Economic General Staff, as such, has no relevance. Ought we, for instance, to raise the income of old age pensioners, or to spend the same sum of money on ARP protection for schools in dangerous areas ? The decision upon that question is not merely a matter of social and economic results, each item of which is highly subjective as a problem in valuation; it is also the deposit of political pressure brought to bear on the Cabinet through the House of Commons and the electorate with which an Economic General Staff, again as such, has no concern.

The proponents of this concept have, I fear, forgotten that supreme maxim of administration that we owe to Sir Henry Taylor, which I have already quoted, 'He who has in his hands the execution of measures,' he wrote, 'is in very truth the master of them.' It is from this angle that we must approach the problem of coordination and planning. There are, I think, two sides to it. On the one hand, there are the large issues of valuation; these, it is obvious, are, in their central context, political decisions that only a War Cabinet can responsibly decide. If it chooses to consult eminent economists about them, whether Lord Stamp, or Sir William Beveridge, or Mr. Keynes, I am only too glad that this should be so. But let us be clear that they are then being consulted, not as

economic experts, but as persons of a large commonsense whose counsel it is worth while to have before
policy is finally made. On the other hand, there are
the decisions which come from the coordination of
the massive details handled by each Department.
These can, I suggested, be dealt with effectively for
presentation to the Cabinet for settlement only by
the men who are immersed in them. You cannot
coordinate unless you are the master of those who
execute your decisions ; and, at this stage, wise decision
is the deposit of intimate acquaintance with infinite
details all of which are familiar to you from daily
handling. That is denied to an Economic General Staff
by the very nature of the conception upon which it is
based. Were it to be tried it would either become as
futile as the Economic Advisory Council—upon whose
grave no serious administrator has been found to shed a
tear—or as annoying as the Cabinet Secretariat under
Mr. Lloyd George, when a number of very able men
continuously interfered with policy with which they
had only an outline acquaintance of a very general kind.

I believe that the proper technique for economic
coordination and planning emerges directly from that
form of Cabinet structure which I discussed in an
earlier part of this lecture. In a fundamental sense, the
essential decisions must be made by the War Cabinet
itself; no lesser body can, subject only to the ultimate
will of Parliament, hope to formulate them with adequate
authority. Below the War Cabinet, there should, I suggest, be an Economic Affairs Committee, which would
be presided over by the Minister for Economic Coordination. The members of that Committee would be the

Ministers in charge of the different departments, with
the Chancellor of the Exchequer, or his nominee, as an
ex-officio member, to represent the Treasury view. The
preparation of the material for the questions this committee would discuss and decide ought to lie with a
committee of the permanent heads of the departments
concerned. From this angle, the effective coordination
of policy would, at each point, be in the hands of those
who were directly responsible for its execution.

The structure that I have outlined will be familiar to
you from its obvious resemblance to the central defence
structure of this country. At the apex of the pyramid,
in each case, is the Cabinet. Below it is a committee,
on the economic side headed by the Minister of Economic
Coordination, and including all the Ministers directly
involved, which corresponds to the Committee of Imperial Defence, of which the Prime Minister is chairman.
I think the former, like the latter, would need a small
secretariat of its own, but this, like the Cabinet secretariat, would be a clearing house, and not an originator
of policy. Below this, again, would be the committee of
heads of departments which would correspond to the
committee of chiefs of staffs. All of them, no doubt,
would form from time to time their appropriate sub-
committees for investigation and report. The merit
of this scheme, as I venture to think, lies in the fact
that it refuses to contemplate the separation of
policy from administration, especially where the
separation results in placing the right to be consulted
in the hands of men who have no responsibility either
for political or administrative decisions. This scheme
avoids a friction that is bound to cause delay. It

places the responsibility for advice and decision squarely where it belongs. It makes the unification of policy the business of those who build its separate parts. There is no reason why any eminent economist, the utilisation of whose services is now pressed so earnestly upon the Government—particularly by other eminent economists—should not be fitted into this structure at a point where his combination of special knowledge and administrative experience would make him of particular value. Since I believe that the effectiveness of an administrative whole is rarely more than the sum of the effectiveness of each of its separate parts, I believe that this scheme meets the needs of the problem that war—and indeed peace also —presents to us, by making those who direct those separate parts responsible for making them into a combination which works as a coherent unity motivated by a purpose growing from within its common life. Such a purpose, in the experience of administrative history, is rarely imposed from without by men who do not share the responsibility for the execution of policy.

5   LOCAL GOVERNMENT

I do not need, I hope, to prove that a living and effective local government is part of the essential framework of a democracy. There is a point beyond which centralisation is not merely incompatible with freedom; it is also incompatible with the very efficiency it is intended to secure. It is no doubt true that war necessitates a far more rigorous control at the centre of affairs than peace permits; obviously, for instance, considerations of finance and of safety from air attack must mean a curb on local initiative. Obviously, also, certain standards must be uniformly imposed, the level of which can be more clearly seen, and therefore more effectively directed, from the centre than from the circumference of government.

I think this is undeniable. And I think it undeniable, also, that in the event of dislocation of the central Government through air raids, something like the system of regional commissioners that has been established becomes urgent for the maintenance of the orderly processes of administration. But it is, I suggest, difficult not to view with alarm the widespread tendency to replace the normal system of local government by emergency committees to which all the effective powers of borough councils and the like have been handed over. They work in virtual secrecy; no public opinion can be formed about their functioning; and from the very nature of their creation they tend unduly to identify the problems of the emergency with the totality of the problems local government has to confront. While I admit at once that their existence is due to the pre-war belief in the imminence of disastrous air raids, these have not yet come; and in the light of this, I suggest that the sooner we return to the classic system the better for our future.

I take this view on many grounds. Everyone admits the value of keeping Parliament in being in wartime, except that dangerous minority which sees in war an opportunity of scrapping altogether the democratic machinery of the state. But every reason for keeping Parliament in being is a reason also for maintaining local government life in its normal way. It means

that what is done is publicly done; it means that
effective criticism is continuously possible; it means
that grievances can be ventilated with some prospect
of remedy. The junta system, as I may term it, has
already shown grave weaknesses. It tends to put
excessive power into the hands of the officials. It
makes the members of the junta inaccessible to the
normal opinion before which a local authority has to
justify itself. It cuts off from effective service in local
government numbers of men and women whose special
interests are not always adequately represented in that
junta. In many areas, particularly in the counties, it
has resulted in the confinement of policy-making to a
single political party whose assumption has been that
nothing matters but the expenditure they cannot avoid
by statute and ARP; indeed it is not an exaggeration
to say that some at least of these committees have
identified ARP with local government so far as their
main work has been concerned. A good deal of the
'black-out' in education and public health since the war
began is, I think, traceable to this unfortunate attitude.

It is a bad system in principle. If it is prolonged,
it means, first, that people will get unaccustomed to
the idea of democratic local government; I do not need
to remind you how dangerous this is. Frontal attacks
on freedom can be resisted at once; the more insidious
attack, which comes from suspensions at first deemed
temporary, are not less dangerous. People, as Hitlerite
Germany shows, too easily forget their rights unless they
are accustomed to their continuous exercise. The junto
system cuts off the electorate from its representatives,
and, from this angle, it has already done grave harm.

It has meant that hundreds of men and women who were accustomed to see that the complaints of their constituents were properly investigated, now lack the means to do so. It means also that hundreds more, who were being trained in the art of self-government by membership of local bodies, above all, by the cut and thrust of discussion in committees, have been forcibly cut off from their training. It means that elected persons with special interests, it may be the library, or education, or maternity and child welfare, have no longer the opportunity effectively to press their point of view. And the repercussion on the officials is bad. Inevitably, with their new and, I admit, overwhelmingly important duties, they tend to neglect whatever of normal local government work is not pressed on their attention. The librarian who is fuel controller tends to forget the new significance in the black-out of public libraries, when there is no committee to watch, week by week, the performance of his normal function. And the official's sense of the urgency of his new tasks tends to communicate itself to the members of the junta in their turn. They begin to think of local government, not in terms of its creative possibilities, but in the much more narrow context of civil defence. If they are bold, one hears them admitting this frankly; the normal services, they say, must take second place. If they are timid, they refuse to take any initiative the impulse to which is not directly communicated from Whitehall for fear of criticism, especially with the omnipresent fear of the rates in their mind.

I hope, therefore, that we shall go back at once to the normal. The London County Council is proposing

to do so; and some, at least, of the London boroughs
are following its lead. Even a three months' suspension
has done grave harm—in education for example. I
cannot believe that we should have had the makeshifts
and hesitations of this period if those on the councils
who know the urgency of education, the dangers which
have already resulted from the postponement of its
influence, had been able to make themselves heard.
If Parliament can meet in war time, local government
bodies can do so as well. No one, I hope, would think
of entrusting Whitehall with unlimited discretion
without that scrutiny to which it is subjected in the
House of Commons. I do not need again to emphasise
the valuable results which have followed from this
scrutiny; and I see no reason to suppose that they
may not be expected in the analogous sphere of local
government. There is the more need for them in the light
of the new functions which have been devolved upon it
since the outbreak of war. For it is a good principle of
administration that, whenever there is reason for the
conference of a power, there, also, is the ground for the
creation of a means for publicly scrutinising its exercise.

6 CIVIL LIBERTY

No aspect of the war is more important or more
delicate than that of civil liberty, and in no aspect,
certainly in a political democracy, is it more urgent
to be vigilant about the powers a government seeks
to obtain. It is not only that the emotions of a war
period make it far more difficult to set boundaries
to legitimate criticism; the famous case of *R. v.
Halliday* in the last war is only the supreme example

of the fact that even the Bench is likely to be affected by their contagion. Even more than the emotions of a war period is it necessary to take account of the inherent tendency of officials, first, to seek for a well-rounded and ample system of control, and, second, to seek its operation in such a way as to ensure the maximum despatch and secrecy in its exercise. Nowhere is the abuse of power so easy, or so dangerous, as in this realm. Every bureaucracy contains foolish men to whom no price is too high for unity in ideas, who are prepared, therefore, rather to suppress than to persuade. I assume that in time of war the duty to speak freely on matters of public interest is more, and not less, important, than in time of peace. On matters like the aims of the war, on the methods of conducting it, on the experience of the administrative process, we need all the light that we can obtain. Silence in these realms means the certainty of error. It means the end of responsible government, for it excludes from the area of those who influence the Government all those who deny its aims and methods. That is the highroad to totalitarian dictatorship.

I cannot seek here to discuss in the detail that is desirable the Defence of the Realm Regulations upon which the Government takes its stand, I can only seek to commend some general principles to you. I begin by admitting at once that certain limitations upon freedom are necessary to the conduct of war. If, as Sir John Anderson has alleged, a political organisation seeks to persuade evacuees to return in order to hamper the Government's power to cope with air raids, there should clearly be authority to deal with such malevolence. If, again, an organisation is found to be tampering with the allegiance of the troops, I agree that the penalty for the offender should be swift and severe. The duty, further, of the Government, to see that such facilities as the postal service are not being used to convey information to the enemy clearly justifies the exercise of special powers over the telegraph and the mails.

This, I imagine, is largely common ground. The problem begins where criticism of the Government begins. What is promoting 'disaffection?' What is 'giving aid and comfort' to the enemy? What is 'hindering the prosecution' of the war? All of these are wide terms, which leave room for immense differences of opinion. Are communists promoting 'disaffection' by insisting that this is an imperialist war? Are fascists 'hindering the prosecution of the war' by continuing their fantastic propaganda against the Jews? Would it be an act of sedition to make a speech at Aldershot complaining of the inadequacy of allowances to soldiers' wives and children? Is the Fellowship of Reconciliation not entitled, as Sir John Anderson seemed to suggest in the House of Commons, to assist conscientious objectors by advising them how best to claim their rights before the tribunals? Ought a citizen to be able to say that he suspects the *bona fides* of the Government? Ought he to be allowed to argue that peace without victory is desirable? What, in a sentence, are the limits of the restraints a Government under war conditions is entitled to impose?

The methods of restraint, in principle, seem to me pretty clear, if we assume that their end must be the preservation of the maximum possible freedom; and I suggest that there can be no other end in a political democracy.

1. The Government must not in any case be both accuser and judge. Whenever, therefore, it is of opinion that a breach of the regulations has taken place, it should be compelled to bring the alleged offender before an independent tribunal which alone should have the power to determine the result.

2. The Government must have no power, in any case, to suspend the writ of *habeas corpus*.

3. The Government should have no power, in any case, of preventive arrest and detention.

4. The Government should have no power, in any case, to deport citizens from one area to another without proof before a tribunal that their activities are a definite breach of specific regulations.

5. The Government should have no power to punish the expression, written or spoken, of opinion unless it can be proved before a tribunal (*a*) that the expression created an imminent fear of public disorder, or (*b*) was giving secret information to the enemy.

6. Any regulations made by the Government under the Defence of the Realm Act should be submitted to Parliament for approval by means of a confirming resolution.

7. No agent of the Government, local or central, should have the power to prevent the exercise of the right of association except where it can be shown that this is likely to lead to a breach of the peace by the holders of the meeting.

8. No regulations should be made by the Government the purpose of which is to introduce industrial conscription or to impede the exercise of the legal rights now possessed by trade unions.

All of these are, I suggest, necessary limitations

upon Government authority if effective political and economic freedom are to be preserved. The laws on the Statute-Book already give ample power to any Government to control that kind of sedition or seditious conspiracy we all desire to control. Power taken beyond the limitations I have suggested is certain to be abused in this war, as it was abused in the last. It is not enough to say that any individual case may be brought up in the House of Commons. The Minister will always protect the mistakes of his subordinates, if necessary, by the use of his majority. A clear *prima facie* case was made out against the police some years ago in the Thurloe Square incident, after an elaborate investigation by an unbiased tribunal set up by the National Council of Civil Liberties; you will remember that the then Home Secretary refused to give any attention to its findings. Government, in the circumstances of war, is capable of unutterable stupidity and indefensible injustice. The need for safeguards against these characteristics needs no elaborate exposition. Without them, whatever the assurances a Minister may offer about his intentions, in the absence of such safeguards stupidity and injustice there are bound to be. Our business is to secure from Parliament the most emphatic procedural devices we can against dangers which may well defeat the purpose for which most of us support this war.

I want, if I may, to add one word about a danger which is real and against which no adequate safeguard at present exists in the law. One political organisation, at least, has found in the exploitation of the pathology of 'racialism' a means of sowing hatred and promoting injustice in the community. This is not a wartime problem merely; it is a problem of peacetime also. I confess that I should like to see an extension of the law of libel and slander to cover cases of this kind. If men go about the country preaching not that a particular person A. B. is responsible for a given evil but that a whole community is responsible therefor, as the law stands, that community has no protection against them. Granted the experience of Germany, I think that protection is important. I think it would be given by conferring on the community concerned the right to bring a representative action against a man or body of men for libel or slander, civil or criminal. If, for instance, Sir Oswald Mosley says that this is a war forced on Great Britain by the Jews, I think he should be compelled to prove in a court of law the truth of his claim, under the usual penalties. There is an interesting legal precedent for such an action in *Brown v. Thomson & Co.*[1], and I think it is a salutary precedent since it seems to have stopped the obnoxious and lying propaganda against which it was directed. I see no reason why the seeds of racial or religious hate should be sown in this country without an appropriate remedy for those who suffer from the hate. If such accusations are true, they must be susceptible of proof; if they are untrue, the sooner the law insists that a penalty shall be enacted for their utterance, the better. It may be that such accusations are a temporary phenomenon due to the grim times in which we live. But German experience proves that there is a Gresham's law in this kind of

[1] [1912] S.C. 359.

propaganda. I should not feel that it was an unwarrantable interference with freedom of expression to penalise our British Streichers before they get well under weigh.

7 FREEDOM *v*. DICTATORSHIP

On any showing, government is a complex art, and the number of those who practise it successfully is small. Even in peace, it is not an easy matter to persuade men to grasp its difficulties; and there is rarely a time when research into its foundations does not become, by the mere fact that it goes deep, a challenge to those foundations. War, by its very nature, throws a blinding light upon them. It tests, as only revolution can test—and revolution is only war in a special aspect—the validity of basic principles. A people that can meet the final test of war and emerge from it with the essential *mores* of its governmental structure unimpaired, can claim, I suggest, to have discovered part, at least, of the secret of why men obey their rulers—the central problem in political philosophy.

And that leads me to the final thing I want to say. From one aspect, this war is a conflict between two theories of government: it has set rule by discussion over against rule by coercion. The German people has been made since 1933 the inert recipients of orders it is its legal duty to obey without scrutiny. There is no way in which it can change its rulers save by their forcible overthrow. Its wants are proclaimed, the validity of those wants assessed, by men who have absolute power in their hands and refuse to admit the common man's right to question the decisions at which they arrive. Public opinion no longer exists in Germany in any sense that has meaning. Those who are ruled have ceased to be ends in themselves. They have become means to the realisation of an end they may not define nor seek, as a process, to evaluate.

We have begun, at any rate, upon a different plane of operation. The supreme contrast between the spectacle Germany presents, and that of our own system, is the intensity of free discussion which surrounds the process of rule. What we are fighting for, whether, indeed, we ought to fight at all, the adequacy of the men and the measures to the ends in view—all these are matters for discussion in the market-place. Such a system obviously presents its difficulties to those entrusted with the power to formulate decisions. They must move more slowly than their rivals. They have to persuade, to explain, to listen to grievance, to seek to adjust it; above all, when they act, they have to justify their action before an audience no small part of which is at least as capable as themselves of judging the worth of their decisions. They know that they risk their power by presenting it for acceptance in the way which rule by discussion demands.

Obviously, this is not an easy procedure compared with that of dictatorship; 'any fool,' as Napoleon said, 'can govern in a state of siege.' Its success depends upon the ability of our rulers to produce in the citizen body the sense that the ends they serve justify the sacrifices they are compelled to demand; and upon the sense, not less urgently, that their methods are just in their incidence upon the population. To achieve that conviction in the mass of citizens in a

D

society so unequal as ours will require all the imagina-
tion and skill of those who are called upon to rule.
It is not in any party spirit that I affirm my own faith
that a democracy wages war the more successfully
the more equal is the recognised interest of citizens
in its functioning. From this I infer the conclusion
that the unity of our nation will be the more fully
maintained the more we move in the direction of an
equal society. A great adventure like war wins the
faith of men in the purposes for which it is waged
by producing in them the conviction that the end
it seeks to reach is worth all they can be asked to
give. Government by discussion is not for the sake
of discussion merely; it is for the objects, also, about
which the discussion takes place. That is why, in
my own judgment, nothing so lifts the morale of a
democracy like ours in wartime as the use of great
authority for the great social changes that are inherent
in the very logic of the democratic idea. Coercive
government means a supine people; democratic
government means a thinking electorate. But if the
electorate is to think, its rulers must respond to its
thought; and the way of response lies through the
gate of equality. Whether it be India or our colonial
possessions, the distressed areas or the unemployed, the
great quality called for now from those who govern, is
magnanimity. Where that is present in a Government,
it has a power of endurance and regeneration which
only overwhelming material superiority can destroy.
In the degree that our rulers learn that lesson we can
be certain of a victorious outcome. Our business is
to see that our rulers learn it while there is yet time.

2

NEW POWERS OF PROPAGANDA AND REPRESSION

HAMILTON FYFE

NEW POWERS OF PROPAGANDA AND REPRESSION

1 THE POWER OF THE LIE

I AM going to ignore the war. In wartime repression and propaganda must be endured up to whatever point is thought necessary. It is of propaganda and repression in peacetime that I shall speak.

The lesson of the last war which sank most deeply into the minds of our ruling class, and especially those members of it which control the Press, was the Power of the Lie. It had not before been realised that the public in hours of tension would swallow any story, no matter how improbable or thinly authenticated. Lying is one of the weapons of war, and I am sometimes in doubt whether to be proud or ashamed of the fact that in 1914–18 we lied far better than anyone else. I need only recall the Belgian children with their hands cut off and the Corpse Factory lie, while for infantile credulity it would be impossible, I think, to beat the widespread belief in the legend of the Russian troops arriving in England during August, 1914.

This discovery of the public's unsuspected gullibility came in very handy towards the end of and just after the 1914–18 war. Ruling classes everywhere had been struck by panic. The Russian Revolution (the real one which installed the Bolsheviks in power) was

the cause of this. Propaganda against the Soviet
system immediately became intensive. There was no
need for the Government to undertake it; the Press
controllers rushed to it of their own accord.

Mr. Humbert Wolfe has satirised newspaper men,
too severely perhaps, in the lines:

> One cannot hope to bribe or twist,
> Thank God, the British journalist.
> But, seeing what the man will do
> Unbribed, there's no occasion to.

I have ventured to compose a similar quatrain
about the newspaper controllers.

> You can't give orders to the British Press
> To emphasise, embroider or suppress,
> To baste the Reds and take a Fascist tone—
> There is no need, they'll do it on their own.

And, profiting by the lesson learned during the last
war, they will do it with a great deal of skill.

Lord Baldwin in 1931 thought he had made the
discovery that

> several newspapers with huge circulations are 'engines
> of propaganda' for the constantly changing policies,
> desires, personal wishes, personal likes and dislikes of
> their owners.

There were two mistakes in that. In the first place,
those who figure as owners of newspapers are most
of them not really owners at all. They are controllers,
but not proprietors. The finance of the Press is so
arranged that while the papers are mainly owned by
shareholders spread all over the country, very few of

these shareholders have votes at the company meetings. They hold, most of them, preference shares, which carry no voting rights. The deferred shareholders, consisting chiefly of the controller and members of his family and friends who have been let in on a good thing, keep all the power. But the peers whose names are connected with the largest circulations are not, as Lord Baldwin supposed, the owners of the papers they control. His second error was to attribute to them the pushing of their personal whims and ideas. They do that very little. It is bad for business. Their propaganda is principally directed against institutions, systems, parties, which Lord Baldwin is as anxious to suppress as they are.

The method they employ is the colouring of news. Let me offer a few examples of the attempt to bring the Russian system into disrepute. Reuter's Agency sent out a Moscow message to this effect:

> Moscow doctors will today examine the three Reichstag prisoners to determine the effect of their long imprisonment on their health.

That appeared in the London *Evening News* (controller at the time, Lord Rothermere) in the following shape:

> Russian doctors, says Reuter, are examining the three men to see what effect, if any, their imprisonment has had on them.

That 'if any' was calculated to make readers say 'All rubbish, of course!'

In the *Daily Express* (controller, Lord Beaverbrook) there appeared during October, 1931, a photograph of a ship discharging cargo in a London dock. It had beneath it the words:

> Unloading cases of gold sent to France from the United States.

Gold was in the news just then. We had gone off it, and, though very few people knew whether Gold Standard was a horse or a dog, yet a picture of this kind had interest. A month later a scare had been started about butter from Russia. It was displacing British butter. It was rancid. Avoid it! So the *Daily Express* republished the dock picture with this caption:

> Unwanted Soviet butter being landed in England.

A party of Russians came on a visit to England. The *Manchester Guardian* described them as

> looking very much like well-to-do Lancashire artisans, sturdy and obviously healthy.

The *Morning Post*, now incorporated into the *Daily Telegraph*, said they

> all had the drawn and hungry look which follows privation and deep suffering.

Those statements in the news influenced opinion far more than leading articles could have done. What passes for a fact is of greater power than any quantity of argument. When people know they are being argued at, they are often distrustful. If a Woman's Page in a newspaper printed an article on the advantages of royalty, it would have little or no effect. But a remark that Queen cakes have come into fashion again as a compliment to our dear Queen makes nine out of ten readers say 'How nice!'

It may surprise you to know that the Woman's Page is often used for propaganda. Indeed, there is no part of a newspaper which is not sometimes so used. Even the astrologers can be pressed into service. At a time when Lord Beaverbrook thought France had too much influence on British policy the *Sunday Express's* Mr. Naylor wrote:

> The stars of France are not the stars of Britain, and the sooner this is realised the better for us. The stars now show that Britain is once again in danger of shouldering new burdens engineered by French diplomacy.

Again, when the paper was complaining that we imported many things we could make at home, its astrologer declared:

> The effect of Uranus will be wonderfully constructive. British supremacy in engineering will reassert itself. The day of foreign importers of household gadgets and industrial machinery is gone.

Those are examples of indirect propaganda. The direct method is seen in the large amount of space devoted to sport, in the puzzles (even *The Times* has its cross-word), in the competitions for which big money prizes are given. Here are inducements to think about things more amusing, and perhaps more lucrative, than politics and social progress. The popular 'national' dailies have almost dropped leading

articles. They report speeches in a few lines only, and
Parliamentary debates scarcely at all. The effect of
this is seen in the low estimation in which politicians
are held (fifty years ago, when their speeches were
reported fully, they were looked on as great men);
and in the impossibility of getting electors to record
their votes. It has another consequence: it is pulping
the public mind—at any rate, a large part of it.

2 THE POWER OF THE POLICE

As time went on and the Russian system survived,
and then actually began to flourish, the propaganda
of the ruling-class Press, which is almost the only
Press we have—was not considered adequate. The
Government felt it necessary to take a hand. Lord
Baldwin revived a Sedition Act of the 14th century.
A Police Act of 1839 was dragged out and dusted, so
that meetings might be more easily broken up. The
Official Secrets Act, as to which the Coalition Attorney-
General (Sir Gordon Hewart) had pledged his word
in 1920 that it could not be applied to the Press, was
invoked against the Press, and when an appeal against
a magisterial decision was lodged, the Lord Chief
Justice (formerly Sir Gordon Hewart) dismissed it,
in spite of what he had promised as Attorney-General.

In fear of the consequences of a vigorous campaign
of protest, the Government, which had refused to
amend the Act, was compelled to do so. But it still
leaves them with new powers, and the other Acts
mentioned above are fully in force, showing how
nervous the ruling class has become, especially about
the fighting services. If it had been suggested during

the later part of the 19th century that sedition might
be spread among sailors and soldiers, the ruling class
would have laughed at the idea. 'Let them try it,'
would have been its reaction. A Kipling story showed
the certain result of such attempts. The feeling of
security which then reigned has fled. Alarm has
succeeded confidence, and as usual has led to harsh
measures of attempted repression.

It was clever of the Tories to rake up old laws.
Mr. Walter Elliott, one of the shrewdest of them, has
said truly that

> if one wants to introduce a new thing in this country,
> one must do it as if it were an old thing.

For example, he went on, it was

> no use wearing black shirts to get the Corporative
> State: that system had already developed farther in
> England than was generally recognised.

So under the Act of 1360 Tom Mann was asked to
agree to be bound over not to do certain things and,
on his refusing, was sent to prison. No proof was
offered that he had any intention of doing the things
in question. What had seemed to be a fundamental
principle of British law was set aside.

An effort was made to apply similar treatment to
the right of members of Parliament to investigate
shortcomings on the part of the Government. Duncan
Sandys, M.P., learned that the anti-aircraft preparations made by the War Office were unsatisfactory. He
took his information to Mr. Hore-Belisha, Minister

for War, and said he proposed to put down a question on the subject. Hore-Belisha, instead of saying: 'Well, my dear fellow, there are deficiencies, but we are overcoming them as fast as we can. Won't you leave it at that?' in which case the matter would have been heard of no more in public, chose to run to the Prime Minister to tell him that Sandys was a naughty boy. Possibly the fact that Sandys was Winston Churchill's son-in-law, and the further fact that the Prime Minister both detested and feared Churchill, had something to do with it—I don't know. Anyway the Prime Minister, instead of telling his subordinate not to be an ass, sent him portentously to the Attorney-General, and that official had the incredible unwisdom to threaten Sandys with the Official Secrets Act. He ought not to have known what he did know! Of course there was a row and an enquiry, which ended in everybody leaving the court without any stain on his character. Repression had not won a victory, but it had been allowed to retreat in good order.

Taking their cue from the Government, the police have, in the words of Sir Chartres Biron, long the chief London police magistrate, 'made more arbitrary use of their powers,' and become, as the president of the Prison Visitors Society put it: 'more autocratic.' They have used an act of 1824 to repress what they call 'loitering.' A journalist going home after his work in the early morning took out a letter and hesitated whether to post it or not. He was warned. A Bank of England clerk was actually taken into custody for looking at cars in a parking place, and the magistrate, though he discharged him, said the policeman had been right to make the arrest. At Cambridge a don named Wooster, who was distributing pacifist leaflets, was spoken to by a constable in a threatening tone; he asked for the man's number, and was at once taken into custody. His request for the policeman's number was described by the judge at his trial as 'unusual'—as if the public were expected to bow meekly when the police exceed their powers.

3 THE POWER OF THE CENSOR

Another use of the Official Secrets Act was frequently made during peace by Government offices, the Admiralty in particular. It was used so clumsily as to cause laughter rather than annoyance, but it was a new thing in the relations between the authorities and the Press. Frequently, almost every week, newspapers received what are called 'D' notices, forbidding them to mention certain matters, which in the public interest it was desirable to keep secret. For example, a 'D' notice was issued by the War Office on Easter Monday, 1939, banning any reference to the defences of Malta. These had actually been referred to in the evening papers for some hours before the ban was sent out at 7 p.m. to the morning papers. It was hastily withdrawn.

Sometimes information which the Press is told not to publish for patriotic reasons is blurted out by Ministers themselves. On 20 March, 1939, a news agency was informed that a naval base in the south of England had received orders to put itself into a

state of 'preparedness.' The Admiralty was asked
about this. The statement was denied. On 25 March,
Col. Llewellyn, M.P., Civil Lord of the Admiralty,
told Weymouth territorials that they had come near
to being mobilised a few days before, thus confirming
the news which the Admiralty had thought too
dangerous for publication.

The worst 'D' notice bungle occurred in April,
1939. In this case the Prime Minister had to accept
the blame. Lord Stanhope, First Lord of the Admiralty,
made an after-dinner speech at a naval port on board
a warship and gave the impression that war was
very near. Reports of the speech reached London
newspapers about 9.30 p.m. At about eleven o'clock
they were asked to withhold these in the public
interest. This request was made by Mr. Chamberlain,
who thought Lord Stanhope had been indiscreet.
The result was to give his remarks far wider publicity,
and to make them seem more significant than would
have been the case if the report had been published
inconspicuously.

As to private pressure being put on journalists to
publish or to refrain from publishing certain news or
opinions, Mr. Chamberlain has admitted that 'advice
is tendered,' while Sir Samuel Hoare has given the
assurance that there is 'never undue pressure.' That
must be a matter of personal judgment. Harold
Nicholson, who has experience both of the Foreign
Office and of journalism, does not deny that in the
giving out of information there may be discrimination
between the perfectly 'trained seals,' which is American
slang for journalists who catch and swallow whatever

is thrown to them, and those who are less well behaved.
He wrote in his book *Diplomacy* :

> In so far as 'guidance' is concerned, it is obvious
> that certain correspondents (whether serving Govern-
> ment or Opposition papers) are more experienced,
> intelligent, and reliable than other correspondents. It
> is inevitable that the former should be treated with
> greater confidence than the latter.

In other words, the correspondent who is reliable
enough to print just what he is told and too intelligent
to ask awkward questions gets more than the troublesome, ill-bred fellow who has opinions of his own.

Was it 'undue pressure' when a Cabinet Minister
rang up a newspaper editor and begged him to beware
of offending Hitler? and when the same Minister
invited a cartoonist to lunch so that he might emphasise
the risks of making the Nazi leader look too ridiculous?
Would not such a Minister be inclined to support a
change in the law which would relieve him of the
need for such blandishments and permit him to issue
ukases instead of making requests? Lord Astor,
though he is a newspaper proprietor himself (he owns
the London *Sunday Observer*, though he does not
control it—Mr. Garvin does that), would favour such
change. He asked in 1938 :

> Is it in the interest of the country that M.P.s and
> writers should have complete freedom to abuse the
> heads of other States, especially at moments when their
> Ministers may be conducting the most difficult diplo-
> matic negotiations?

Already MacDonald in 1935 had spoken of the
possibility of 'fresh powers to curb the Press,' while

a Tory M.P. (de la Bere, Evesham) suggested a
Government newspaper to counteract the discreditable
tendencies of the others. It was the anxiety to spare
a foreign dictator the knowledge that he was despised
and detested by the British nation which inspired
the wish for Press censorship. This was not the first
time that an attempt had been made in this country
to suppress criticism of a foreign ruler. In 1852 the
House of Lords debated Press attacks on Napoleon the
Little, Emperor of the French, who gained his power
and kept it by means very similar to those which
Hitler employs. Tennyson, not yet Laureate, replied:

> My lords, we heard you speak: you told us all
>   That England's honest censure went too far;
> That our free Press should cease to brawl,
>   Not sting the fiery Frenchman into war.
> It was our ancient privilege, my lords,
> To fling whate'er we felt, not fearing, into words.
>
> If you be fearful, then must we be bold;
>   Our Britain cannot salve a tyrant o'er. . . .
> What, have we fought for freedom from our prime
> At last to dodge and palter with a public crime?

As poetry deplorable, the sentiment is sound and
as necessary for us to cultivate now as it was then.
Even more necessary, for the forces we see ranged
against us are larger and more formidable than they
were in the middle of the last century. There are
hidden hands stretching out in many directions to
filch freedom away from us. We have not yet given
in to them as Denmark had to do when the Nazis
took offence at a statement by Richard Acland, M.P.,
as to a Czech woman having a swastika branded on

her flesh, being reprinted in a Danish journal. An abject apology had to be inserted and the editor dismissed. We have not, I say thankfully, sunk so low as that. But repression in various new forms has been busily at work even here.

An issue of a weekly paper called the *Leader* was banned by the Retail Newsagents' Federation on account of some reference to Hitler which the authorities found distasteful. That was in November, 1938, when Mr. Chamberlain was trying to make effective his 'dearest wish' that he and Hitler might remain on friendly terms. Shortly before this a newsreel item, showing Wickham Steed, a former editor of *The Times*, and A. J. Cummings, the popular *News Chronicle* columnist, speaking a few words each on the crisis, had been withdrawn at the direct instance of the British Government, which informed the American Ambassador that it might have a prejudicial effect on negotiations that were then in progress. Mr. Kennedy passed this on to the *March of Time* agent in this country, and the item was cut out.

The Government, through the Prime Minister, speaking in the House of Commons on 1 December, 1938, tried to pretend that this had not been done for a political reason. He 'was not aware,' he said

of any instance in which the removal of parts of films had been asked for by the Government on political grounds.

But Sir John Simon had a week earlier admitted that the Ambassador had been approached by the Government, and Sir Samuel Hoare, following Mr.

E

Chamberlain in the debate on 1 December, contra-
dicted his chief, and said the item was objected to
'because it might have inflamed the atmosphere.'

That may have been the motive for the change of
mind by news-reel film companies when ex-President
Beneš paid a visit to Cambridge to address the Liberal
Summer School. The idea of making a film was
dropped. Further, the title of the address was altered
from *The Future of Democracy* to *Politics as Science
and Art* at the bidding of some hidden voice, and the
police refused to allow Czech refugees to gather outside
the hall of meeting to greet their patriot leader.

Most disquieting of all these repressive incidents was
the one recorded by Wickham Steed in his Penguin
book on the Press. On 9 October, Hitler

> placed his veto upon the return to office of three prominent
> British public men. When this news was broadcast,
> the whole nation was moved to wrath. Of the depth
> of its wrath hardly a hint was given next morning in
> the leading British newspapers, some of which were
> almost apologetic. Enquiry into this humiliating behaviour
> on the part of our 'free Press' elicited the information
> that certain large advertising agents had warned journals
> for which they provide much revenue that advertise-
> ments would be withheld from them should they play
> up the international crisis and cause an alarm which
> was bad for trade. None of the newspapers thus warned
> dared to publish the names of these advertisement
> agents or to hold them up to public contempt.

This statement caused naturally a good deal of stir and
denials were freely offered, but Steed did not retract,
as he certainly would have done, being an honourable
man, if his charge had been proved to lack foundation.

4   THE POWER OF THE PEOPLE

I hope I have now shown that both propaganda designed to prevent people wanting to criticise or attack the Government, and measures to repress such attacks or criticism when they are, in spite of propaganda, delivered, have increased in recent years under Tory rule directed by Lord Baldwin and Mr. Chamberlain. May I discuss for a few moments how Socialists should react to assaults so barefaced on freedom of speech? First, let me say that much Government propaganda is useful and necessary. When Departments issue explanations of new laws, or news about what steps are being taken to improve things, or even on rare occasions warnings that certain facts had better be kept quiet, no objection need be raised. Sometimes departmental publicity is used for the glorification of a political chief with a taste for the limelight. That should be vigorously discouraged—as it usually is by the guilty party's colleagues in the Cabinet!

In general direct communications from Government offices to the Press are undesirable. When the offices have anything to communicate, newspaper men can be asked to receive it, and editors can decide whether to publish it and in what form. Government publicity has increased largely of late. The instalment of a publicity agent at Buckingham Palace opened a new era in this direction. To stop it altogether would be scarcely possible, and indeed, as I have indicated, not entirely desirable. But Socialists have thrown upon them the responsibility of improving their own methods of instructing and persuading the nation. These have been neglected in the past, and still are capable of much improvement. The London County Council election in March, 1938, marked high water so far in the Labour method of appealing to voters. It is no secret that the services of very talented advertising men were enlisted, and 'what they said went.' Their motto was 'Nothing but the truth,' but they put it in attractive guise, and the result was all that could be desired.

Socialist propaganda must be honest, and must not be afraid of making the facts known. A good many Labour people think this ungentlemanly. They seem more anxious to stand well with the other side than with their own. The right kind of education would get rid of that—the kind that the Left Book Club, and in many districts the Workers' Educational Association or the National Council of Labour Colleges are providing. We have the majority of elementary and secondary school teachers with us, and they do their part in spreading the light, so far as they are able. We have a large proportion of civil servants, too, who will be of the greatest use when the switch-over to Socialism comes. There will be no difficulty with the BBC, if present trends of opinion among the various staffs of that institution do not alter. Among the mass of the nation we can recruit fresh millions as soon as we set energetically about it. We have an overwhelmingly strong case, which must prevail if it is driven home to the mind of the nation in an effective way.

3

THE UPRISING OF INDIAN AND COLONIAL PEOPLES

LEONARD BARNES

THE UPRISING OF INDIAN AND
COLONIAL PEOPLES

1 DOUBTS ABOUT EMPIRE

THE events of the last two or three years, with their
record of discontent and rioting among colonial
peoples, even more, perhaps, the series of official
reports inquiring into the causes of these events, have
untuned that old rhapsody in red, white and blue, to
which our imperialists delighted to listen, and in
whose magic melodies they thought they heard the
beat of progress towards social liberty and welfare.

> If we are prepared to fight to keep our colonies
> we must be ready to strive to the utmost to clear our
> title of deserved reproaches.

So ended a recent article in *The Economist* which
was devoted to expressing remorse for the past mis-
deeds of empire and to searching for means of atonement
for them. Even to the city of London, even to the
very temple of imperialism, there has penetrated at
last the realisation that the colonies are a reproach.
The King, in his Empire Day broadcast, said

> It is only by adding to the spiritual dignity and material
> happiness of human life in all its myriad homes that
> an Empire can claim to be of service to its own people
> and to the world.

The facts of colonial life show beyond all cavil that this is precisely the service which the British Empire is failing and has long failed to render.

Recognition of this truth is spreading—or was spreading until the war began. When on 7 June, 1939, the House of Commons debated colonial affairs, the official attempts to strike the customary note of complacency were literally howled down.

Mr. Josiah Wedgwood said that the past year, in his view, had been the worst, the most damaging to British prestige, the most inciting to riot and disorder, that he had ever known in political history so far as the Colonial Empire was concerned.

When Mr. Malcolm MacDonald, Colonial Secretary, sought to present the Empire as the inviolable home of universal peace, freedom and justice, it was, significantly, a Conservative member, Mr. Bracken, who described the speech as the attempt of a maiden aunt to explain the facts of life to a sophisticated nephew.

The unwillingness of the House to boast of the British as the best of all possible empires was in surprising contrast to its usual temper on these occasions. There was, perhaps, nothing odd in one Conservative member comparing Italian rule in Libya and Rhodes favourably with British colonial rule; there are plenty of Conservatives ready to admire Italian methods anywhere. It was surprising, however, that a Liberal M.P., criticising the ban on the local Labour Party by the Government of Mauritius, should ask 'Is that the freedom and liberty which are flourishing throughout the Empire?' and add that British rule in Cyprus today was worse than that of the Turks sixty years ago.

Other members, too, invited the Colonial Secretary to study French colonial rule, particularly in the West Indies, and to bring our own up to the French standard.

These strictures are not all. In some sections of opinion in our ruling groups there is even a glimmering of a remedy.

If the pace of internal development in the colonies is to be quickened, it can only be as the result of assistance given in the form of free grants.

Such was one of the conclusions of Lord Hailey's *African Survey*.

The basic trouble is diagnosed in this way. In many colonies riots and disorders have revealed a situation of economic dislocation which it is beyond the power of local administration to resolve. Faced with the need for heavy expenditure to lessen the impact of poverty, unemployment and ill-health, colonial administrations are compelled to levy heavy taxes, which, in turn, make the economic deadlock more insurmountable than ever. Last year the expenditure out of the various colonial budgets exceeded seventy million pounds, of which almost exactly half went on administration, debt and defence. Much of the money so spent is raised by heavy duties on the imports of almost all the necessaries of life. In the colonies themselves there is neither money nor authority to carry out the schemes that are needed to save them not only from social distress, but also from continued political discontent and unrest.

This being so, direct assistance to colonial budgets is clearly due from the British Treasury on the items

covered by administration, debt and defence. Poll
taxes and food taxes should be abolished. The fiscal
approach to the rich, whether persons or companies,
should be much less timid. An end should be made
of the anomalies by which, for example, gold-mining
companies on the Gold Coast pay no tax into the
colonial exchequer, but are liable to British tax.
Most important of all, steps should be taken to ensure
that the wealth which colonies produce should be
applied to increasing the well-being of their inhabitants.
At present the most important colonial products belong
entirely to capitalists, alien to the colonies concerned,
who have imparted the capital necessary to develop
natural resources. The equity in such concerns is
wholly owned outside the colonies, and their value to the
colonies is merely a wage and taxation value. So long as
such conditions continue, it will evidently be impossible
for flourishing internal markets to be developed.

Apart from these monopolistic terms of exchange
of colonial produce—terms which ensure that the
'native' engaged in production receives only a small
share of the wealth he produces—the mass unrest
in the colonies has two other main economic roots.
One is the primitive character of productive methods
involving low output per man. And the other (which
is sometimes, though not always, linked up with the
first), is the width of fluctuation in the prices of tropical
products. Since 1930 tobacco has fetched as much
as 1s. 3d. a lb. and as little as 3d.; sugar as much as 40s.
a cwt. and as little as 4s.; rubber more than 2s. a lb.
and less than 2d. Such price-spreads are apt to be much
greater than those of European products. In earlier times

the bump caused by fluctuations of such magnitude was much softened by the resilience of the peasant economy. In the colonial empire the British have by now for their own purposes largely destroyed the peasant economy. Slumps today are therefore much more directly creative of colonial revolt than they used to be.

It is in the British West Indies that economic changes have had the most striking and far-reaching political consequences. There the colonial governments have been obliged to consider and frequently to adopt all sorts of steps to meet the demands of the workers, for example land settlement (an attempt to recreate the peasant economy), minimum wages, public works, slum clearance, old age pensions, workmen's compensation. The most discussed issues in the recent past centred on the aspirations of the middle class, and were concerned with federation of the scattered islands and with elective control of the colonial legislatures. Today these matters still find prominence, but they are desired in the interests of the masses, and even greater attention is given to adult suffrage, the break-up of the big estates and the creation of a cooperative peasant community, the nationalisation of the sugar factories and public utilities, the provision of old age pensions, health and unemployment insurance, and industrial reform.

Even to draw attention to these obvious facts is usually regarded as revolutionary socialism. It is, therefore, the more surprising to find *The Economist* suggesting that

> what is needed most of all is the supply of capital in equity form rather than in the shape of prior charges,

to bring to colonies the manufacturing, processing and refining industries which will lessen their too exclusive dependence upon agriculture on the one hand and mining on the other. The whole plan must be bound up with the evolution of new methods of cooperation between imperial governments and private enterprise, in the supply of capital and in its control and management. And what is needed finally is to foster those forms of economic progress which will enable colonial populations to contribute in greater measure than they have done so far to the upbuilding of capital resources themselves.

If all this were really meant, if our rulers were genuinely determined to make free and large-scale gifts of capital with a view to developing colonial resources and encouraging colonial wealth to accumulate in social ownership in the colonies, instead of being drained away to swell the private incomes of a handful of rich men and powerful corporations in this country —why, then, colonial status would be at an end, and the knell of imperial domination would indeed have sounded. There would be no need for any uprising of the colonial peoples; they would be uplifted by the City of London turned good Samaritan.

2 THE CLAIM OF CONGRESS

On the whole, however, it seems likely that there will still be work to do for the movements of national-democratic revolt in the provinces of Empire. Of such movements the pattern and the prototype is the Indian National Congress. Everyone knows that the Congress is a great organised power dedicated to freeing India from British domination. It is not a party; it is much more even than a coalition of parties. It is a complex of interests and movements which draws its membership and its strength from all classes, from Brahmins and Untouchables, from rich and poor, from employers and workers, from landowners and dispossessed peasants.

Thus it is a really national front, bearing a real resemblance to the national front which the Chinese have built to withstand Japan's aggression, or to the *Frente Popular* with which the people of Spain met the challenge of Mussolini and Hitler. It gains cohesion from being able to converge against an alien overlordship. It is also actively and almost desperately engaged in reconstructing Indian social and economic life. And, finally, it has to reckon with the Franco's of India, the so-called native Princes whom British authority has suborned to spike the guns of the Indian independence movement.

The Congress is therefore one of the great driving forces of progress in our day and generation. Taking its rise from a religious rebirth and a liberal tradition dating from before the Mutiny, the Congress first met as such fifty-four years ago in 1885. Many years passed before it came to adopt political independence as its major objective. Just as the workers who carried out the general strike in Jamaica last summer always began their meetings and demonstrations by singing 'God save the King,' so effusive professions of

loyalty and attachment to the Throne, unswerving allegiance to the British nation, and a firm resolve to stand by the Empire at all hazards and all costs were common form in the Indian Congress until after the Great War.

Since then things have moved rapidly. The Congress is now for full independence outside the British Empire. For several years under its aegis the common people have been fighting for civil liberties and democratic rights all over the sub-continent. After the bringing into effect of the new Constitution in 1937, Congress assumed governmental office, or shared it, in eight out of the eleven provinces of India. In those eight provinces much has been done to widen civil liberties in spite of the interference of Governors, though even in such provinces the people have found it well to keep the Congress Ministers continually alive to their demands and to the promises made to them —as in Bombay, for instance, where the workers had to declare a one-day protest strike against a Congress-sponsored anti-trade union Bill, and were fired on by the police for doing so.

Two of the most impressive evidences of popular awakening have been the formation of peasant mass organisations throughout the country, and the rising spirit of militancy in the trade unions. Both types of organisation have been closely linked with the Congress, and in consequence Congress has undergone great changes in the last two or three years. Its membership has risen from some 600,000 to over 5,000,000. Alongside the old nationalism of middle-class intellectuals there has grown up a huge mass movement of peasants and workers.

Nor is this mixture of nationalist and class struggle confined to British India. It has been carried over into the India of the princes. The feudal and oppressive character of the princes' rule, and the need for a measure of democratic criticism and control, are too well known to call for comment here. The agitation in the States is both a spontaneous movement among the States peoples themselves, and also a phase of the struggle for power in the federal India of the future. To secure that the federal representatives of the States should be democratically elected by the States peoples, and not the mere nominees of the princes—this was a vital issue for the Congress, so long as there was a prospect of the federal part of the 1935 Constitution being brought into force. It might have decided whether the federal scheme was to be introduced with Congress cooperation, or in the face of a vast renewal of civil disobedience. With the advent of the war, some weakening of the princes' authority has become essential to the survival of any democracy in India.

Indian democracy has extended its activity and its self-confidence along another line also. I refer to the astonishing increase in India's awareness of the world crisis and of the part which a free India might play in the solution of it. Under Congress leadership the Indian people have become more and more eager interventionists in world affairs. They have sent their medical unit to China, boycotted Japanese goods, and called out Indian workers from Japanese mines. In spite of their own deep poverty and distress, they sent food, materials, and even some men to Spain. The entire weight of their mass national awakening has been thrown on the side of democratic freedom, and against imperialist aggression.

In recent years, in short, the popular forces in India have set a noble example to those of Britain. They have clearly recognised the essential unity of these great struggles, and they have proclaimed with no uncertain voice their willingness to stand shoulder to shoulder with us in the common labour for the people's power and the peace of the world. On us in Britain, therefore, lies a special and a huge responsibility—to bring to an end the oppression and exploitation wrought in our name upon the four hundred millions of Indians.

On the other hand, the internal difficulties of Congress are great and perhaps increasing. Equally difficult are the relations of Congress with the Moslem League. In the sphere of provincial administration, the Congress Ministries have done much. In the release of political prisoners, in the prohibition of drink and drugs, in education, in relieving the peasants of some of their heavy burdens, even in improving the condition of workers in industry, though this has proved the hardest task, their record has been no discreditable one. But even before the war began there was a growing feeling that they had already exhausted most of the possibilities open to them under the new Constitution. They were, moreover, under the troublesome necessity of keeping up anti-imperialist feeling among their supporters, while at the same time producing the modest results as administrators which were all that the Constitution left open to them.

Again, the Congress leadership has undoubtedly reacted somewhat unfavourably against the militancy of the workers and peasants. The Red menace has been freely used to frighten Ministers responsible for law and order. The trade unions and peasant organisations have been represented as standing for violence, and as therefore incompatible with Congress ideals. Gandhi has sponsored the doctrine that the class struggle is unethical and un-Indian, and that landlords and employers should be looked on as trustees of the interests of their employees and tenants. Subhas Bose was ejected from the President's chair because he opposed these extravagances of the moderate men, and because he was suspected of that worst of all crimes in a modern popular leader, namely wanting to give a fighting lead to the workers.

Twenty-five years ago India supported Britain's crusade to destroy German militarism and to make the world safe for democracy. Gandhi and the other Indians leaders fell into the trap. They rendered every help they could to the British power. As a result, India was bled white. Not merely the monstrous waste of Indian man-power and of the material resources of a poverty-stricken people, not merely extreme economic exhaustion, but the crawling orders of General Dyer, the massacres of Amritsar, and the Rowlatt Acts were the bitter fruits that Indian garnered from her chosen 'loyalty' in 1914.

It was an expensive mistake. India will not make it a second time today. For twenty years now she has been struggling against the British power for that self-determination which the British victory in 1918 had pledged in words to all weaker nations. Year by year since then the British power has fought the Indian liberationist movement, imprisoning its

F

leaders, illegalising its organisations, and firing on
its processions. Of the terrible reconquest of India
in 1930 and the years that followed, our present
Foreign Secretary, Lord Halifax, was one of the chief
instruments. From the nature of the case, India sees
much more clearly than the people of this country
what is the true character of our new war. She knows
that a Government which holds her own four hundred
millions in bondage cannot be trusted to fight for the
liberties of any people. ('We embarked on war,' said
Mr. Chamberlain in the Commons on 12 October,
'simply in defence of freedom.')

Hence the phrases of the statement on war policy
issued by the Congress on 14 September stab their
way very painfully into the conscience of every British
democrat.

> The Governments of Britain and France declare that
> they are fighting for democracy and freedom against
> aggression; but their past history is full of betrayals
> of proclaimed ideals. The last war meant secret treaties,
> Versailles, and enlargements of Empires. In Manchuria,
> Abyssinia, Czechoslovakia, and Spain, aggression was
> encouraged, democracy betrayed, and collective security
> sabotaged. The League of Nations has been killed.
> . . . It would be an infinite tragedy if even this war
> is carried on in the spirit of imperialism for the purpose
> of retaining the very structure which causes war. . . .
> If Britain fights for democracy, then she must neces-
> sarily end imperialism, and establish full democracy in
> India.

Which of us will not flinch before the accusing
finger of those words? They throw out a challenge
to the political faith and good sense of the British

people more formidable even than Hitler's challenge
to the armed strength of Chamberlain's Government.
They point inexorably to India as the touchstone of
British war aims. Give India full self-government
with the right of secession now, and our profession of
concern for freedom in the world will have at any rate
one leg to stand on. Withhold freedom from India now
and this war adds yet another to our lengthening list
of 'betrayals of proclaimed ideals'; the British people
will have fallen into the same trap that Gandhi fell
into in 1914.

3 THE DEAD HAND OF BRITAIN

How have the British Government answered India's
call to declare their war aims in general, and as applied
to India in particular? With an uncompromising
negative. Lord Zetland, the Secretary of State for
India, has spoken more than once on the subject in
the House of Lords. The first time he plaintively
lamented, where he might have rejoiced, that the
Congress declarations 'were couched only in abstract
terms.' The second time he curtly observed that
Congress had chosen an unfortunate time to assert
its 'claims, and even had the hardihood to add that
the British Government would be more willing to
listen after India had given it some reason for gratitude.
This wretched and mean-spirited approach has now
been fully confirmed by a statement of the Viceroy,
Lord Linlithgow, published as a White Paper on
18 October 1939. The statement postpones for the
duration the whole issue raised by Congress, declines to
attempt any definition of British war objectives, and

proposes to set up a consultative committee, composed of various parties and groups in India, to assist the Viceroy in the prosecution of the war.

Moreover, the British Government have added injury to insult in a number of ways. Without Indian consent they have declared India a belligerent country; they have sent Indian troops on active service overseas in spite of the protests of India's elected legislators; they have passed an India Act Amendment Bill by which the democratic powers of the Provincial Governments survive only on sufferance from the Viceroy.

Congress has not made its mind up hastily on the question of Britain's wars. The whole problem has been exhaustively examined and discussed in annual conferences over a series of years. Considered resolutions have been passed whose meaning leaves no room for ambiguity. Opposition and hostility to any war calculated to preserve Britain's status of imperial privilege in the world have been repeatedly declared. India will strike, and strike hard, for her own freedom, if such a war is forced on her. She will not bargain, but will settle accounts with her British oppressors once for all. No other interpretation than this can be placed on the Congress resolutions on war. India has already made its first gesture of protest by the resignation of the Congress ministries.

The Linlithgow statement puts great stress on the British Government's desire to lay down after victory 'the foundations of a better international system.' Some sanguine observers assume that in the alleged prosecution of this alleged aim India will be wholly on the British side. But India will want to know what the phrase 'a better international system' means in the mouths of men who destroyed the League of Nations and would not build a peace front with the Soviet Union. By what precise steps is such a better system to be attained? Neither Chamberlain not Linlithgow has any answer to questions like these. Even if they had, the grand remonstrance of the Congress would remain valid—

No refashioning of the world can succeed without the solution of the Indian problem.

India, indeed, is the key to the whole colonial question, and an inescapable issue for the architects of any new international order, precisely because she is the keystone of the imperial arch. To assist her to immediate self-determination would be an act of faith and justice that would transform world politics more thoroughly than any war waged to preserve our Empire system. It would herald the end of imperialism, even if the comprehensive abolition of colonial status in places like tropical Africa had to wait some decades. Or, to put the same thing in another way, it would involve a shift in the balance of class-power in Britain that would tell decisively in favour of the unprivileged majorities in every country in the Empire.

For these reasons it will be fatal if the people of Britain allow themselves to be led away into sanctioning the repression of Indian aspirations for full democratic freedom. British rule in India has perfected the technique of such repression during many generations. It will try—indeed is trying—to split the popular ranks by setting Moslems against Hindus and the native princes against the struggling democratic forces of British India. Congress, as the strongest and most firmly anti-imperialist political organisation in the sub-continent, it will seek to tame by alternate cajolery and threats, by Dyer-like violence interspersed with false promises and a few unreal and insignificant concessions.

The business of democrats at home is to forewarn and forearm themselves against these methods, to use their own political and civil rights to make such treatment of India impossible, and to assist actively India's efforts to shake off the dead hand of British rule, whenever they may be made and however inconvenient their occasion from the standpoint of British warmongers and the British ruling class.

4 THE COMMON CAUSE AGAINST MONOPOLY CAPITALISM

I spoke of the Congress as a National Front. It is typical of colonial liberationist movements everywhere in the sense that it gives voice and shape to certain aspirations of the whole Indian people—the depressed and exploited workers, the land-hungry and debt-ridden peasantry, the disillusioned and frustrated middle classes. Because of this inclusive character, because it is a genuine cross-section of Indian society, and seeks to hold the various and often conflicting elements of that society together for the purpose of united and concerted action, it is a difficult team whose management calls for supreme qualities of statesmanship. United action is only

possible for it along one single line, the line of resistance
to foreign overlordship, for the simple reason that
that line coincides with the only interest common to
the whole composite membership of Congress. Whenever it deviates from that line, there is an immediate
loss of cohesion in its ranks; the compound mass tends
to fall apart into its constituent elements, and the one
common purpose becomes lost in a cloud of sectional
objectives, many of which are mutually discrepant.

In other words, the tendency of the British empire,
like that of other empires, has been to recreate in
India the same general structure of social classes as
has been characteristic of British society itself.
Industrial investment in colonies requires at least a
rural and, later, an urban proletariat, and the empire
builders are quick to improvise such classes, if need
be, out of the most recalcitrant material. The process
inevitably gives rise to conflicts of class interest
similar to those with which we are familiar in our own
country. Those conflicts are continuously developing
and working themselves out in Indian life, as it were,
parallel to the life and activity of Congress, and
sometimes even inside them. They cannot be effectively tackled, let alone finally solved, until after the
main anti-imperialist objective of Congress has been
gained. It is the task of Congress to prevent their being
brought to a head before victory on the anti-imperialist
front has provided the conditions for their solution.

But while this latent and occasionally active struggle
within the ranks of Congress has to be recognised
and understood, it would be a cardinal mistake to
think of Congress as an unholy alliance which, without

any honest unifying bond, comes together cynically
and arbitrarily to pester and blackguard a well-meaning
if obtuse British authority that somehow seems to
have outstayed its welcome in India. There is a very
solid and material basis for a national front of all
classes against British rule, and it consists simply in
this, that the British connection, as it is called,
includes a monopolistic exploitation through trade and
investment of the Indian economy as a whole. India
itself as an economic organism is subordinated to the
monopolist privileges of alien capital, and therefore
all ranks in Indian society have an interest in bringing
this general subordination to an end. Political
independence is the first decisive step along the road,
but it is only the first.

Here then is the economic *raison d'être* of Indian
liberationism. The need to dispossess foreign capital
of its coercive powers cuts across, complicates, and
for the time being overrides the internal class friction
set up by the industrialisation which the empire system
imposes at the colonial end. If this were not so, the
national question and the social question would
merge, and colonial liberationism would take shape
simply as a proletarian and socialist movement. As
things are, however, large sections of the colonial
middle class, well-to-do farmers, middle-men, industrialists, even money-lenders and land-speculators,
have economic roots which link them with the struggle
for national autonomy.

Hence one of the distinctive features of 20th
century social development, the rise of movements
of national-democratic revolt at the outposts of

empire which seek alliance with the democratic and socialist forces in the colony-owning countries with a view to bringing under social control the great monopoly combines that form, as it were, the power stations feeding the whole imperial process. In the years immediately ahead of us it may well be that the main offensive against the monopolists may be developed by the colonial independence movements rather than by the older working-class organisations at home.

However, that may be, it is of the first importance that the democratic movement in Britain should never for one moment forget that the monopolists who generate power for the imperial process are the same monopolists who have determined the armaments policy of European governments, who have devised and operated the schemes for planned restriction of output of most staple commodities, who have divided up the markets of the world among themselves, and who are even now running the wartime controls of fuel, power, iron and steel, chemicals, foodstuffs and the rest, to which this country has lately become subjected. These monopolists may be unscientifically but adequately defined as the City, the Lords, and the Federation of British Industries. They man the last citadel of our collapsing and bankrupt economic system, and they are the ultimate enemies of democracy and socialism: British progressives and colonial nationalists have an equal and a joint concern in securing their fall from power. It is the plainest of commonsense for us to collaborate with Indians and Africans to that end.

For imperialism is not a policy which the monopolists happen to have selected from a number of choices open to them, and which they can abandon in favour of some non-imperialist policy if and when the spirit moves them. To imagine that any such possibility exists is to assume that the politics of imperialism can be divorced from the economics of imperialism and lead an independent life of its own. But it is surely self-evident that you cannot have monopoly in the economic field combined with pacifist, non-aggressive, non-annexationist policies in the political field. Monopoly is from its first conception built on compulsion and restriction. It is the extreme of privilege and the diametrical opposite of freedom and equality.

It is therefore constitutionally incapable of fighting either as the champion or the ally of democracy. Imperialism *is* monopoly and monopoly *is* imperialism : the identity between the two is full and exact. Men do not create the vast monopolist structures of the modern world from sheer moral obliquity, or even because they seek the aesthetic satisfaction of the architect. They create them because in modern conditions profit cannot be reliably safeguarded in any other way.

5 COLONIAL INDEPENDENCE

The solution of the colonial question thus provides the solution of the social question at home, and *vice versa*. Both solutions consist, quite simply, in the democratisation of monopoly, in converting the banks and trusts from strongholds of private and anti-social

interests to instruments of public welfare—in sub-
jecting them, that is to say, not merely to public
control, but also (a very different matter) to popular
control.

Here, then, is our aim; and the character of the
aim governs the character of the means by which
we move towards it. In dealing with this great and
complex Empire issue, and its modern accompaniment
the uprising of the Indian and African peoples, we
do not need to worry our heads overmuch with Open
Doors, mandate systems, have-not powers, new
international share-outs, joint trusteeships and the
rest. Phrases like these are either red herrings, or
stand for matters of quite secondary importance.
For democrats in Britain the colonial question means
one thing and one thing only, namely planning and
using the most effective machinery of cooperation
with the colonial liberationist movements for the
ending of British political and economic domination
in colonial areas. This involves a very clear recognition
of the fact that we as democrats have no part or lot
in the apparatus of imperial rule, and wish to have
none. We should give up thinking of ourselves as
guinea-pigs to the conservatives in this matter of
colonial government.

In particular do we need to view with deep suspicion
all proposals for the administration of colonies by an
international body. No one suggests that India should
be internationalised. Why should any other colony
be so? All colonial peoples hate the very notion of
being governed by an international combine. And
they are right, because the notion only occurs to

minds that approach the whole issue from the wrong end. The problem is not to redivide the advantages of colonial possessions among European nations; it is to see that colonial wealth is distributed equitably to the 'natives' who produce it instead of to European shareholders.

The way out lies through colonial independence and the shift of class-power in the home country which that implies. International control, in the sense of extending the mandate system and so on, will go by the board. True, colonial independence by itself is not enough, and its workability in practice will depend on the creation by the people's power in the western democracies and the Soviet Union of some quasi-federal alliance which the liberated colonies might enter. But that topic, supremely significant though it is, lies beyond the province of this essay.

4

NATIONALISM AND DEMOCRATIC SOCIALISM

R. H. S. CROSSMAN

NATIONALISM AND DEMOCRATIC SOCIALISM

1 ANGLO-SAXON MISCONCEPTIONS

IT is, I think, the special function of the Fabian Society to examine objectively and critically the ideas of the Left and to ensure that socialist policy is not vitiated by false presuppositions. Unfortunately no parties are more conservative of ideas than Labour Parties; and nowhere is this clearer than in the attitude of progressive people in this country to the problem of nationalism. That is why I have chosen to tackle this subject today; and I would say in advance that, if I stumble against certain cherished illusions, the action is deliberate. You may be able to cherish illusions and defend the status quo; but a socialist who is not prepared to be clear-sighted at the cost of hurt feelings is in a bad way.

Let me start then by asserting that the cult of 'Internationalism' in progressive circles in Britain and America has been, on the whole, disastrous. The sweeping condemnation of nationalism as essentially vicious, the accusation of imperialism levelled at anyone who seeks to defend his country's interests, the superior contempt for patriotism—all these high-minded attitudes may be excellently suited to the domestic politics of a great power, but they come to very little when they are made the basis of a foreign

policy. It has been the fashion of late to contrast
the policy of the Left, as founded on principle, with
that of the Right as founded on interest, as though
principle and interest were mutually incompatible;
to denounce 'power-politics' and laud League action,
as though the latter could abolish the former; and to
assert that the mainspring of Labour policy was peace,
though in fact any foreign policy at all implies
an acceptance of war under certain conditions. All
these easy slogans were harmless as long as Britain
and France, with other League States, held an
unchallenged superiority of power. And they had
the supreme convenience of an ambiguity so profound
that they could unite in a single movement pacifists
and believers in the use of force. Unfortunately, this
ambiguity resulted in profound confusion as soon as
the rise of Nazi Germany provided a test of their
practical utility. We are still suffering from the results
of this confusion.

But at least, now that we are at war, we know that
we are confused; and that is a great advance. The
next step is to clear the confusion up and to discover
the foundations on which a sober and constructive
socialist foreign policy can be built.

Let me start with a memory of the Labour Party
Conference at Bournemouth in 1937. I can still
remember the rather jejune debate on rearmament,
livened only by the brilliant irrelevance of Mr. Aneurin
Bevan. James Walker rose to wind up, among the
audible sniffs of the Left, who sensed that he would
almost certainly make a bloomer. And he did! He
actually asserted that there was more freedom under

the Union Jack than in most parts of the world. This was too much for the militants. A full-throated snarl of disgust rose from the floor.

This scene has always stuck in my memory. Mr. Walker had uttered a platitude. But he was howled down not for uttering a platitude but for recognising the Union Jack as his flag. He had committed the solecism of expressing pride in British institutions; he had broken the tradition that 'progressive' people always run down their own country.

This animus against patriotism is an important part of Left ideology. It makes much of our socialist thought not 'international' but anti-national and develops naturally into inverted nationalism. The same people who shudder at the Union Jack grow ecstatic when they see the flags of China, Spain, Abyssinia and above all of Soviet Russia. Having disowned their own country, they adopt another and become fervent advocates of its most extravagant claims.

Once again an illustration may help. The other day I was lecturing to a working-class audience on Soviet diplomacy and had pointed out the extreme 'realism' of M. Molotov. When I had finished, an intelligent Trade Unionist got up and said 'The Russians feel that there is in the USSR something of eternal value, which must be defended at all costs. This justifies any and every measure of diplomacy, however ruthless.' It did not even occur to him either that there might be something of eternal value in Britain worth defending, or that, if there was, he would be the first to denounce any ruthless measures taken by a British Government. He had simply

G

transferred all his patriotism to the USSR. Though he did not realise it, he displayed the very Jingoism 'my country right or wrong'—which he regularly denounced as vicious nationalism.

To this inverted nationalism, we must add a third characteristic, blindness to the significance of power. Left ideology fantastically over-estimates the importance of public opinion and under-estimates that of strategy in international affairs. It assumes that the pressure of good-will will bind together our friends and that moral censure will deter our enemies. For many years after 1918, a socialist who soberly studied the problems of military and naval strategy or of commercial power was suspect. Power-politics, it was felt, had been abolished and would stay abolished so long as progressive people continued to disregard them. If the peoples all really believed in peace, there would be no war.

How deeply this peculiar brand of pacifism had infected the Left was shown by its reaction in the spring of 1936 to the semi-militarisation of the Rhineland. Dislike of French 'nationalism' combined with a general feeling that Germans should be allowed to do what they liked in their own country, prevented any realisation of the strategic importance of this move. That the building of the West Wall would make collective security infinitely more difficult was grasped only by a small minority. The same thing happened in the case of Czechoslovakia. The ethnic side of the Sudeten German problem was given prime importance; the strategic interests of Czechoslovakia were alluded to infrequently and with a feeling of discomfort. For these were felt to be a matter of power-politics, or even of imperialism, with which a socialist could not, with a good conscience, concern himself—unless of course they affected the USSR.

Neglect of the factor of power, a neglect or even repudiation of British national interests, and an excessive attachment to the national interests of other adopted states—these are the three prejudices which have compromised the foreign policy of many socialists. It is noteworthy that all of them could only have grown in a country with a long history of immunity from attack and of national cohesion. They are not, for instance, defects of Russian communism, which has always recognised the prime importance of power, and has never let humanitarian enthusiasm for foreign causes blind it to its own interests. On the other hand they have been widely influential in the Dominions and in the USA, whose security has been even greater than our own, and in the smaller democracies, which could not rely on power to defend themselves in any case.

2 NATIONALISM AND DEMOCRACY

If we are to advance beyond the chaos of national sovereign states, it will not be through the momentum of a movement infected by such prejudices. Mere dislike of patriotism creates no international order. Neglect of British interests is regarded abroad not as unselfishness but as hypocrisy; and as for the inverted nationalism which approves of everything Russian and nothing English, it does not even deceive the British electorate. To plan the future, a socialist movement must understand the past and recognise that its primary responsibility is to its own countrymen. Above all it must grasp the fact that nationalism, if its excesses have been disastrous, has been one of the great civilising influences of the world and is still to-day essentially connected with democracy.

The American War of Independence and the French Revolution were the first great expressions of the idea of national democracy. In these movements and in the theories of the philosophers connected with them two tendencies predominated, the demand for national self-determination and the demand for individual freedom, and these two demands were intimately connected. The earlier democrats realised, far more clearly than their successors, that the political institutions necessary to guarantee the rights of private conscience and enterprise could only grow in a community inspired by a deep sense of unity; and they saw in the nation precisely the community they desired. Thus the creation, in the USA and in France, of the sense of nationhood and of the belief that every individual, whatever his station, was a participant in the life of the nation, was as essential a part of the democratic revolution as the establishment of representative institutions. Nationalism was a force ranged on the side of progress against the supra-national despotisms of the 18th century monarchs; and throughout Europe, with the exception of its western fringe, it remained a progressive force right up to the Peace Settlement of 1918. Germans and Slavs, who had not achieved national unity, recognised more easily than the British and Americans

its vital importance to civilised life, precisely because
they did not enjoy it. The French, too, retained the
Jacobin tradition unchallenged, for the simple reason
that a common frontier with Germany meant that
their national independence was always in danger.

So long as democrats continued to recognise the
interdependence of national unity and individual
freedom, they were in no danger of neglecting the
importance of 'power' in international affairs. No
one for instance who had taken part in the unification
of Italy could suffer under the illusion that public
opinion was the dominant factor either in domestic
or in foreign affairs. He was bound to recognise that
individual freedom was only possible within the severe
limits imposed by the need of national unity, and that
national unity could only be achieved and maintained
by a shrewd manipulation of the balance of international power. Security both at home and abroad
was rightly assumed to be a prerequisite of freedom.

Unfortunately two waves of Utopian ideology swept
over the democratic movements of the world. The
first was the Liberal ideology of the British middle-
classes, and in particular of the nonconformist churches.
Concerned in domestic politics with the demand for
freedom of religious practice and the destruction of
Anglican privilege in education, the British Liberals
gradually evolved an anti-authoritarian philosophy
which fitted admirably with the doctrines of *laissez-
faire*. Progress, they felt, would be achieved by the
destruction of power and privilege and the substitution
of representative institutions. They used Parliament
less to turn the powers of the state to communal

uses than to prevent the growth of any state at all.
So too in international affairs, it was not so much
the misuse of force as the use of force which they
condemned. 'Destroy the old ruling classes,' they
argued, 'and the peoples of the world will live in
friendship together.' Already, in the philosophy of
John Bright, we can see that Utopian belief in the
power of good-will, that vague suspicion of 'power-
politics,' that confidence in disarmament as the
universal panacea, which was to become the *motif* of
later Labour politics. Already in the flagrant contradictions between Mr. Gladstone's electoral denunciation
of imperialism and his practice when he became Prime
Minister, we can see the fate which was to dog every
progressive Englishman when, instead of criticising
the users of power, he came to use it himself.

The deep public reaction against the adventurers who
precipitated the Boer War only strengthened this Liberal
ideology. While the actual rulers of the country, whether
Conservative or Liberal, practised conventional diplomacy, progressive opinion, so long as it was in political
or intellectual opposition, became not only anti-national
and anti-impressionist but 'anti-power.' It began to
attack that sense of national unity and national discipline upon which the whole structure of our liberties was
built, and to dream of a time when, power-politics and
nationalism abolished, the peoples should live at peace.

These illusions were the peculiar characteristics of
British Liberalism, though they were also influential
in the USA and in the Scandinavian states. But the
second ideology, which now became popular, captured
the élite of the Labour Movement all over the world.

This was the Marxism of the members of the Second International. The Socialist theorists rightly exposed the inadequacy of national democracy in a world of monopoly capitalism and economic imperialism. They showed that the democratic sense of national unity among the peoples of the Great Powers was being used both to confirm the internal position of the new plutocracy and to further its ambitions abroad. With great acuteness they analysed the economic structure of the nation-state and the new factors which finance-capitalism had introduced into international relations. They saw that, with the new mechanised warfare, national independence could no longer be maintained by the courage of a citizen army, since power now depended not only on the discipline of the soldier but on the control of heavy industrial plant. In future a Great Power would mean a state with financial resources and with industrial wealth either in its own territory or inside its empire, or obtainable from others during a blockade by the enemy; while the independence of the smaller powers, particularly if they were economically backward, would become more and more of a fiction, so long as national sovereignty was maintained.

The analysis of the Marxist theorists was of first-rate importance and remains even today the basis for any understanding of modern society. But when we turn to their positive philosophy and practical programmes, we are faced by a number of loosely connected illusions, not dissimilar from those of the British Liberals. Believing in the possibility and necessity of the world revolution, they assumed that in due course the whole system of nation-states would disappear, to be replaced by world socialism. This enabled them to content themselves with mere denunciation of imperialism and power-politics. They did not ask themselves how they would themselves manage a nation-state because they thought they would never be called upon to do so.

In the second place, they tried to substitute the international solidarity of the working class for the national solidarity of the early democrats. Obsessed by the factor of class conflict, they predicted that proletarian unity would of itself prevail against the antiquated structure of the nation-state. With the destruction of the bourgeois class would come the destruction of the nation-state and of imperialism.

Though the Marxist theorists fiercely attacked the Liberals for their Utopian disregard of power-politics, and based their analysis of the state exclusively, and quite erroneously, on the concept of class power, the effect of their positive programmes was to strengthen Liberal illusions. Power-politics was now admitted to dominate human affairs and intense moral indignation was aroused against it. Nationalism was dismissed as mere hypocrisy, patriotism reviled as the betrayal of working class solidarity. The Labour movement was given a simple picture of the forces of darkness at war with the forces of light and a millennial hope of a day when light would triumph. Meanwhile they were taught to eschew those things which are evil.

Thus the foreign policy of Socialist parties in opposition became a strange blend of class-war analysis and pacifist quietism. More and more the Socialists became content to prove the iniquity of the international order and to condemn it *in toto*.

Marxism provided a scientific reason for complete inaction combined with moral indignation. By condemning power-politics, it sapped the will to power. Only in the Syndicalist and Bolshevik movements was the old revolutionary vigour still strong.

Even worse, the members of the Second International were infected with a deep hypocrisy. On the platform they condemned nationalism, imperialism and power-politics: in industrial life they were busy claiming a share of the prosperity which depended on these very things. Their Utopian theories were completely at variance with the daily life of a working class movement whose liberties and standard of living were a product of that national democracy which they denounced. This hypocrisy was especially evident in Germany, Holland and France: in Britain it took a different form as the Labour Movement had not thrown off the Liberal ideology of Cobden and Bright.

3 THE PEACE SETTLEMENT AND THE RISE OF RACIALISM

One result of these Liberal and Marxist illusions was that the Labour Movements of Western Europe failed to grasp the significance of the peace settlement. That three antiquated Empires in Eastern Europe had collapsed and that a democratic revolution had taken place seemed of small account to people who already regarded national democracy as the chief enemy of civilisation. That millions of peasants had won their freedom and were busy partitioning *latifundia* and clearing away the remains of feudalism meant nothing to Labour Movements which had long since forgotten

the horrors of agricultural servitude. The peace
settlement was judged chiefly on its treatment of
Germany; and quite soon it became the mark of
the progressive mind to condemn the treaties as mere
products of power-politics, which must be revised as
soon as possible. This analysis was naturally popular
in Germany where nationalist propaganda was already
busy painting a picture of an innocent Germany
despoiled by the thieves of the West. Nor did the
Communists, who had special reasons for hating the
democratic revolution which was thwarting their
Balkan ambitions, hesitate to add their protests to
those of the Liberals and Social-Democrats of the
West. The Green Revolution was permitted to peter
out without any radical solution of the agricultural
problem, and the new states of S E Europe, without
mutual cohesion or assistance from the western
democrats, became for the most part puppets of the
diplomacy of the Western Powers. Only Czechoslovakia,
with its well-balanced economy, and Turkey, after
its nationalist revolution, showed signs of a vitality
which could survive the stresses of the future.

One of the great stumbling blocks in the way of
progress is the difficulty of mutual understanding
between democratic movements in different stages of
social evolution. The peasant movements of Bulgaria
and Croatia, for instance, could have understood without difficulty the ideas and policies of the American and
French Revolutions; but they lived in a world utterly
different from that of the British and French Labour
Movements, or for that matter of the Austrian Socialists
whose Vienna was an isolated outpost of western ideology.

To the Balkan peoples the indissoluble connection between national unity, individual liberty and peasant
proprietorship seemed as self-evident as it did to Tom
Paine : to western industrial workers it had no sort of
significance : to the Communists, it was an outworn
ideology which must be ruthlessly crushed. Once again,
as in 1848, the democratic revolution failed to reach
completion, but this time the western democrats
failed to show any concern over its failure.

The rise of Nazi racialism can only be understood
against this background of Eastern European politics.
For racialism, and with it fascism, is the ideology of
resentment against the failure of the Liberal and Socialist
movements to provide that basis of national and social
security without which individual liberty is meaningless.
Whether we examine the philosophy of Herr Hitler or of
the Rumanian Iron Guard, we shall discover that it is a
reaction against the failure of Liberals and Socialists to
grapple with the problem of unfavoured peoples, or of
classes excluded from consideration by the modern state.

But why, if racialism is an Eastern European growth,
should it have first taken root in Germany? The
answer to this question discloses another aspect of
the failure of the peace settlement. The effect of
Germany's defeat in war and loss of foreign assets
was that she was brought down to the level of a minor
power. She suffered the ignominy of financial control
by foreign creditors; and compulsory disarmament
gave her the psychology of a backward country
without the military sinews of independence. Thus a
nation with enormous industrial resources and the
technical and administrative experience of a western

power became susceptible to that revolutionary racialism which arose naturally in the backward peasant
states when the democratic revolution failed. Anti-
semitism, for instance, is inevitable, and to some extent
revolutionary, in Rumania and Hungary, where the
Jews have taken the place of a native bourgeoisie. Its
basis, however, in post-war Germany, was not the status
of German Jewry, but the inferior position of Germany
as a nation *vis-à-vis* the Western Powers. Relegated
to the economic and international status of her backward neighbours, Germany assumed their backward
ideology—an ideology, which, in its own natural
conditions, could never obtain world importance.

The second reason for the adoption of racialism by
the Nazis is the condition of the Austro-Germans after
the break-up of Austria-Hungary. Deposed from their
position as *Herrenvolk*, they were forced to live on an
equality with, or even in subjection to the people they
had always considered as their inferiors. The national
democratic movement of the Slav peoples had necessarily
acquired a racial colour from long years of cultural
oppression by the Germans. It had come to concern
itself less with the emancipation of all than with the
winning of privileges for this or that racial minority.
Equality of treatment, not for each individual but for
each cultural or racial group, had become the dominant
political ideal in Austria-Hungary, with the result that
the two complementary demands of the early national
democrats, national unity and individual liberty, were
obscured. In their place grew the notion of the
nationalities-state, whose 'democracy' consisted not in
individual freedom but in the equilibrium of rival groups.

It was against the concept of racial equilibrium and the practice of Slav supremacy that the German minorities were induced to revolt. Once again the Green Revolution had failed, the social basis of a new democratic order in Eastern Europe was removed and the chronic economic instability and financial dependence upon the West made it natural that they should reject the idea both of democracy and of the League and look elsewhere for salvation. Inevitably they looked to Germany as their spiritual home : equally inevitably the ideology which excited their devotion was neither the watery internationalism of the west nor Russian communism, but the reaffirmation of the idea of the German *Herrenvolk*, of the ancestral right of Germans not to equality within a nationalities-state but to unity with their brothers inside the Reich and supremacy over the Slavs among whom they lived.

The appeal of racialism was intensified by the weakness both of the League ideology and of the succession states thrown up by the peace treaty. The western democracies had shown no interest in consolidating the gains of the Green Revolution. They tended to regard the succession states as useful outworks against German or Russian expansion, and as democracies on the western model. Fearful of competition, they made no effort to solve the agricultural problem by the encouragement of modern techniques or of industrialisation. Instead they were content to establish the League of Nations and to maintain the fiction that this political superstructure was sufficient to guarantee both security and peaceful change. Alone of the backward countries, Turkey, by a violent national revolution and under the control of a far-sighted dictator, achieved both the national unity and the economic conditions for successful democratic development. And Turkey did this by violating every canon of western liberalism and western socialism.

4 THE DYNAMIC OF RACIALISM

Only if we bear this historical development in mind can we understand the power of racialism. It has three origins. The first is the revolutionary reaction of a peasant proletariat against a Jewish bourgeoisie; this is crude anti-semitism. The second is the racialism of the Slav national democratic movements caused by the cultural and political supremacy of the Germans in Austria-Hungary. The third is the resentment of Germans inside Germany against their subordination to the Western Powers and of German minorities outside Germany to their incorporation in Slav 'nationality-states.' From these three sources arises the philosophy of the *Herrenvolk*, while its dynamic power is due to the social instability of the post-Versailles world.

But German racialism drew fresh vigour from two other sources. In the first place it incorporated in the Nazi movement those elements which had supported the old Pan-German movement. It attracted, that is to say, not merely the unsatisfied poor but the unsatisfied rich, and offered to German industrialists a convenient weapon both for domestic and for foreign policy. This new strain of Prussian imperialism, however, which was of immense importance in the early days of the régime, has steadily declined as the social revolution gathered pace in Germany. Although the conservatives gave Hitler the Chancellorship and at first restrained his revolutionary ardour, the 'Revolution of Nihilism' (to use Dr. Rauschning's phrase) has destroyed the basis of their power; and with their power has gone their ideology as well. Nazi policy is now inspired not by the cautious, hard-headed power-politics of Prussia, but by the revolutionary fanaticism of race.

The second source of vigour was the weakness of western liberalism and socialism. As we have seen, the Western Powers failed to utilise the peace settlement for the completion of the democratic revolution in eastern Europe, contenting themselves with the establishment of 'nationalities-states,' and neglecting altogether the fundamental agricultural problem. Both here and in Germany, Social-Democracy was no more successful. Side-tracked by the success of the Communists in Russia, the militants demanded a proletarian revolution, while the orthodox Labour leaders confined their vigour to a suppression of the militants and the defence of trade union interests within the limits of finance-capitalism. The failure of British Labour in 1931 and of French Labour in 1936 repeated that of the German Social-Democrats in 1918. It was suspected that the Labour Movements were not the representatives of the people in their struggle for advancement, but of one special interest, the trade union movement, while the Communists were the representatives of Russia.

It is my contention that this failure of the Left to maintain its revolutionary dynamic is largely due to its ideology of class conflict and internationalism. The strength of the early democrats lay in their conviction that they stood for the nation. They were prepared both to defend it against foreign foes and to fight for the freedom of its citizens in domestic affairs. This double objective gave them a will to power and, not less important, an understanding of its significance. The modern working-class leaders have neither of these. Internally they accept their position as one interest among others, while in foreign affairs their collective pacifism has been strong enough to effect no peaceful change, weak enough to encourage any aggressor to call their bluff. Losing its sense of national responsibility the Left lost its sense of power.

It was precisely this weakness of Socialism which Herr Hitler perceived. He knew, of course, that the vested interests of the Right could be induced to betray national for the sake of private interests. Now he saw that the democrats of the Left could be put by their own ideology into such confusion that they would be unable to resist him in the initial stages of his advance to power. Their propaganda for peace, revision of the treaties and the abolition of power-politics could become a weapon of aggression. By appealing to the conscience of the west, the leader of the *Herrenvolk* would contrive its destruction. Instead of making a frontal assault, he would invite his opponents to abdicate in the name of justice.

Racialism, like every other revolutionary creed, draws its strength very largely from the weakness of the *ancien régime*, whose antithesis it is. The absurdities of its philosophy carry conviction, because the upholders of civilisation have betrayed their own principles, and failed to build a civilised society. Those very tasks of domestic and European reconstruction which we should have carried out in the name of social justice, are now being accomplished in the

name of racial imperialism. The national control of
the means of production, which we proclaim, is a fact
accomplished by the Nazi war machine, the international planning of economics, which we have hardly
dared even to think of, is now being undertaken by
the closed imperialism of the racial state. No wonder
that Hitler and Stalin can do business together.
Each controls a revolutionary movement, whose
success is due to the failure of western democrats to
complete their own democratic revolutions.

5   CONCLUSION

If the above analysis is correct, several conclusions
of practical importance can be drawn. In the first
place, the miscalculations of Hitler and Stalin, which
precipitated this war, are not wholly disadvantageous to
the cause we stand for. For years there has been a war
on : but one side fought while the other talked of peace.
This period of bloodless aggression is now closed. Against
our will, we have been forced to fight for our lives.
We can only be thankful that the bloodless aggression
did not continue until we were too weak to fight.

In the second place, I am convinced that the Racial
Revolution has already passed its zenith. Reaction
against our lamentable failures gave the Nazis their
chance : the wild extravagance of their politics is now
producing a reaction against themselves, just as
Stalin's search for 'security' is beginning to endanger
his own position. Slowly the conditions are arising for
a new democratic movement against the old plutocracies
and the new totalitarian empires. The peoples of the
world are beginning to feel the need for national and

H

individual emancipation from the 20th century despots and oligarchs. If the burden of the old Leviathan was great, that of the new Leviathan is infinitely greater.

In the third place, if we, as Socialists and Democrats, are to play our part in this new revolutionary movement, we must clear our minds of a lot of illusions. We must admit, without shame, that our first task is the defence of British liberty, and recognise that Europe can only be saved by an Anglo-French cooperation, both economic and military, which must last long after the war is over. We may hope for changes in Germany and Russia, such as will turn them into peaceful powers with whom we can cooperate. But we cannot reckon on that, and we must be prepared to maintain such collective strength, that neither we nor those neutrals who may collaborate with us shall again be subject to a period of bloodless aggression such as we have lately endured. To make our peace aims hinge on a friendly revolution in Germany is futile : we hope and work for one, but we dare not count on its coming.

Lastly, until we admit the indivisible connection of nationalism and a vital democratic socialism, all talk of Federal Union is futile. The aim of any federation, which really arouses loyalty, will not be to destroy nationalism, but to save national unity from destruction by the totalitarian empires. The aim of Democratic Socialism, if Democratic Socialism is to revive, will be not to abolish the nation-state, but to organise those nations who care for civilisation into a federal alliance, complete enough to resist external aggression, and so economically united that they can cooperate for the achievement of a common standard of living.

5

THE DECLINE OF CAPITALISM

G. D. H. COLE

THE DECLINE OF CAPITALISM

1 CONTESTANTS FOR WORLD POWER

THERE are serious inconveniences in living in an age of transition—especially for those of us who are middle-aged. If Wordsworth had been older at the time of the French Revolution, he might well have written, not 'Bliss was it in that dawn to be alive, But to be young was very heaven' but rather 'Cursed was it in that dawn to be alive, But to be middle-aged was very hell.'

For it is in the nature of periods of transition that their problems are unintelligible in terms of the categories to which people are accustomed. When we try to explain them in these terms they make nonsense—we find ourselves hopelessly at sea as soon as we try to put two and two together. It sounds pretty enough to declare that we are engaged today in a war for 'democracy versus fascism'; and some of us would dearly like to feel able to equate the 'war for democracy' with a war for democratic socialism against fascist dictatorship. But in order to make any such equation we have to leave out capitalism and to treat the distinction between capitalism and socialism as irrelevant. We have to leave out the fact that ever since 1917 the Soviet Union has been fighting a world 'war' for communism against capitalism, and that the Soviet Union, basing

its idealogy upon this conflict, is by no means prepared
to accept capitalist 'democracy' as its natural ally.

To this some make answer that fascism *is* merely
capitalism in its imperialist form. Fascism, we are
told, is simply capitalism on its final defensive-offensive
struggle against the irresistible march of socialism.
So it may be, up to a point. But the argument is
unduly simplified. It rests on the assumption, first,
that fascism can be sufficiently defined in purely
economic terms, and secondly that fascism is a static
system, in the sense that it will consent to stand
still while we analyse it—which is by no means the
case. As against this contention that fascism is
capitalism, we are met with the counter-assertion that
fascism and communism are both forms of totalitarianism, and that between them there is no essential
difference. They are, it is argued, natural allies against
the cause of individual liberty. Again, the argument
is not wholly devoid of meaning; but it assumes that
fascism and communism can both be defined in purely
political terms, irrespective of the economic realities
which underlie their political constitutions and methods
of national government and international behaviour.

If, dismissing these easy identifications, we say that
there are, under the conditions of today, not two,
but three contestants for world domination, and that
these three are fascism, communism and democracy,
again we miss out a vital factor; for where, in such
an analysis, does socialism come in? We cannot
identify it with any of the three others. Communism
is undoubtedly, in its economic basis, a form of
socialism; and those socialists who are not

communists but believers in a democratic socialism based on, and carrying to a logical conclusion, the conquests of western parliamentary democracy, cannot accept a classification of world tendencies which lumps them indiscriminately together with the adherents of an obsolescent capitalist system.

Shall we say, then, that there are not three, but four, contestants for world power? That comes nearer to the truth; but as all the contestants are children of one age, and must of necessity adapt their organisation to its requirements, it is not surprising that they should reveal many overlapping characteristics. Because they do overlap in this way, the battle between them quite naturally fails to make simple and obvious sense for those who contemplate it with minds coloured by the outlooks and attitudes of an age that is rapidly perishing as mankind enters on a new stage of technical development and adaptation to a changed scientific environment.

2 CAPITALISM IN EXPANSION

Throughout the 19th century, the two dominant tendencies of growing thought and action were capitalism and nationalism—and these two tendencies continually overlapped as capitalism shaped itself within national units and nationalism adapted its growth to the requirements of capitalist industry. Capitalism grew up in the main within national units as national capitalism, unifying and superseding the localism of the pre-capitalist era. But in face of the immensity of technical development, it was impossible for capitalism to rest within these national frontiers; and so, in the course of the century, nationalist capitalism turned more and more into expansive imperialism under its urge to subdue the world with the new forces at its command. It sought, first markets for its surplus products, and then concessions for the investment of the spare capital of its wealthier classes. In its need to expand production it went further and further afield in search of new sources of raw materials to feed its hungry industries, whose manufactures poured back into the countries which supplied it with primary products of every sort and kind. Trade and 'the Flag' pursued each other all over the globe; and which was following which it was a puzzle to say. Overseas investment played, on an ever-increasing scale, the role of empire builder to national capitalism; and the less developed regions of the world fell helplessly under the sway of one or another of the great powers which had armed themselves with the weapons of exploitation.

For a time this expansive process enriched the world. In the imperialist countries it doubtless enriched the wealthier classes more than the others; but some part of the material benefits of world exploitation fell to the share of the working classes in the form of higher wages and improved conditions of labour, or of a flow of cheaper foodstuffs from the new countries that were being opened up. But, more and more, imperialism led to clashes between the more advanced states, as the struggle for spheres of exploitation and influence became more intense; and presently, under stress of keener competition to sell goods in the markets of the less developed countries and of rising interest rates sustained by the expansion of overseas investment, serious maladjustments began to appear. In Great Britain, for example, from about 1900 the workers' standard of living ceased to rise; the new flow of gold from South Africa increased prices and thus reversed the tendencies of the previous epoch; wages lagged behind prices, and the standard of living began to fall for the mass of the people at a time when overseas investment was increasing faster than ever. Of course, long before this the process of world exploitation by national capitalism had led to a gross disproportion in the distribution of wealth; but it made all the difference when the workers found that they were no longer getting any benefit at all from the further development of the capitalist system. Socialism, which had been in the first half of the 19th century—in Chartism, for example—essentially a hunger movement of the very poor, reappeared from the 1880's onwards mainly as a movement of protest against the extremes of riches and poverty, based no longer on the starving masses at the bottom of society, but rather on the better-paid sections of the working class. For those sections which, by means of organisation in trade unions and the steady development of collective bargaining, had been able to wrest for themselves a share of the increasing wealth of capitalist society, were the first to resent the reversal of the secular tendency for the standard of living to improve. As long as the expansionist phase of capitalism lasted, which it did broadly up to 1914—though it was already being checked for some time before that—this revived movement for socialism remained basically a movement for social reform within the capitalist system rather than for a complete change in the economic basis of society. To the extent to which it sought the socialisation of industry its aim was mainly that of using piecemeal socialisation as a means to social reform, and for the improvement of the standard of living within the existing social order. Hence the characteristic reformism of the Second International, of the Fabian Society in its earlier days, and of the Labour Party in Great Britain—and hence the similar tendencies of the Social Democratic Parties in the continental countries, despite their use of Marxist slogans taken over from the revolutionary age. The old revolutionary socialism survived only here and there, where the shoe of capitalism pinched hardest. It existed as Syndicalism in the Latin countries, as Industrial Unionism among the emigrant workers in the United States, and as Bolshevism in backward Russia, with its exotic large-scale capitalism planted in the midst of a peasantry still subject to the tyranny of an unconquered feudal system. But in the age that ended in 1914 revolutionary socialism was never a world force; it could not become one as long as capitalism was still going strong and remained in general an expanding and creative system.

3 CAPITALISM IN DECLINE

The World War of 1914–1918 upset the already precarious balance of capitalist forces. It interrupted foreign trade and compelled countries deprived of their normal supplies to set up industries of their own, even where these were bound to be uneconomic on grounds of natural unsuitability or the narrow limitations of the domestic market. It permanently destroyed, for certain of the advanced countries, markets, especially in the Far East, which they had held largely for historical reasons. Thus, if the cotton industry had developed as a new industry in the 20th century, no one can possibly suppose that it would have become centred mainly in Lancashire : it would undoubtedly have settled rather in areas offering abundant supplies of cheap labour, such as India, China and Japan, and the Southern States of America. After 1918, Great Britain had to face the irrefragable fact that a large part of Lancashire's market for cotton piece-goods was gone for ever. In the years after the war, with the creation of new states and the determination to preserve, even at high cost, industries established during the years of warfare, new barriers of tariffs, customs regulations, currency systems and so on, were erected all over Europe ; and the revival of world trade was further impeded by war debts and the attempt to exact reparations from the defeated countries, while refusing easy entry of their goods into the markets of the victors. There was, moreover, in the post-war period, first the isolation of Russia from the world market and her disappearance as an exporter of primary products, and then the challenge of the new economic system which was being painfully constructed by the Soviet Union in face of every possible obstruction that the capitalist countries could contrive to put in its way without intolerable economic losses to themselves.

For revolution, that common aftermath of war, came not in the more advanced capitalist countries, which showed themselves better able to stand the strain of prolonged warfare, but in backward Russia, where the capitalist system had irretrievably broken down. Revolution would probably have followed in Germany, in an economic as well as in a merely political form, but for the blockade imposed by the Allies and the fear that an attempt to establish a socialist system might merely call down further measures of vengeance upon the German people. As things were, communism, inverting under pressure of counter-revolutionary forces Tsarist methods of dictatorship and centralisation, established itself on the frontiers of western capitalism and threw the western capitalists into a panic mood of defence against the 'Bolshevist menace.'

In face of these difficulties, post-war capitalism was precariously reconstructed over the rest of Europe. But post-war capitalism exhibited very significant differences from the capitalism of the pre-war period. In one industry after another the capitalists had learnt, under pressure of war conditions, the advantages and the necessity of combination, both for sharing out the limited supplies of raw materials and shipping space, and for presenting a united front in negotiations with the various governments. When the war ended, these lessons were not forgotten. Capitalist organisations, built up as agencies of state control, remained in being as trusts and combines, or as close associations of profit-seeking entrepreneurs, for making the best for capitalism of the post-war situation. In face of the dislocations of the post-war market these bodies turned in increasing numbers to policies of systematic

restriction of output, and even to the deliberate
destruction of productive capacity in order to restore
profit-making on a narrower basis. Capitalism was
learning to worship scarcity, whereas in its expansive
19th century phase it had worshipped abundance as
a means to profit—the more so because it was conscious
all over the world of unexploited markets in which
it could dispose of its surplus products without lowering
the investors' returns. Moreover, whereas before
1914 most Governments had reprobated trusts and
combines as contrary to the free spirit of private
enterprise, in the post-war period they turned more
and more to endorsing the restrictive policies of the
capitalists in order to avoid the further dislocation of
industry through competitive selling in a limited
market. These conditions applied especially to Great
Britain, because of Great Britain's high degree of
dependence both on the world market in general
and in particular on industries at which wartime
developments had struck an exceptionally severe
blow. For Great Britain had sunk a very high proportion of her capital in a narrow range of industries
which found themselves after 1918 confronted, for a
variety of reasons, with exceptional difficulties in
disposing of their products. The restrictions on world
trade damaged British shipping and shipbuilding
severely. The rise of industry in the Far East hit hard
at the textile industries. Technological changes
administered serious blows to the British coal trade—
and so on, through one after another of the leading
British industries. But although Great Britain was
the most obvious sufferer, very similar conditions

prevailed elsewhere. It became plain that capitalism, in accordance with Marxist prophecy, was turning rapidly into a fetter on the further development of the powers of production.

Meanwhile in Germany, which had been prevented from adopting socialism, but was unable, in face of the strength of the socialist movement, to be anything like a hundred per cent capitalist in policy, there developed the stalemate of the Weimar Republic. This created an economic situation, aggravated by the exaction of reparations and the inflation which followed on the French occupation of the Ruhr, in which the phenomena of decaying capitalism were painfully manifested in the ruin of the middle classes and the persistence of unemployment at an intolerably high level. These economic conditions combined with the sense of aggrieved national pride to create a powerful fascist movement; and they were able to do this the more easily because parliamentary institutions and democratic habits of discussion and mutual tolerance had much weaker roots in Germany than in Great Britain. Just as Italian fascism was victorious because of the paralysis of socialist and capitalist forces in post-war Italy, so, a dozen years later, a similar paralysis brought the Nazis to power and ended the depressing experiment of the Weimar Republic.

Over this period, communism, finding itself too weak to carry through the world revolution for which its leaders had hoped, was consolidating itself behind its national frontiers, and killing off or exiling the revolutionary idealists who were unable to reconcile themselves to the abandonment of their larger hopes. Under stress of the fear of foreign intervention designed to crush the socialist experiment, and also of the need to repress idealism within its own territories lest the policies of the idealists should provoke capitalist attack, Soviet communism grew more and more totalitarian in its methods of government. It failed to bring about the victory of communism in Germany under the influence of the depression; and the struggle between German social democracy and German communism resulted instead in paralysing the resistance of the German working classes to fascism, which was thus able to come to power as the reputed saviour of Germany from the Bolshevist danger, but in reality as an assertion of the joint will of the capitalist and nationalist forces to overcome the creeping paralysis to which the country was subject. It is a moot point how one ought to distribute the blame for the weak resistance of the German working classes to fascism between social democratic indecision and communist disruptiveness; and as I have discussed this matter at length elsewhere I do not propose to go into it now.

Wherever the blame lies, the effect of the collapse was to discredit democratic socialism, which was disastrously weakened by trying to fight simultaneously on two fronts—against the more violent forms of capitalism on the one side and against communism on the other. This attempt to face both ways led to a paralysis of the will-power of social democracy—a paralysis which can be seen in other countries besides Germany—by no means excluding Great Britain. In

Great Britain, however, the great strength of the economic foundations of capitalism—a legacy from the days when Great Britain was in truth the workshop of the world—enabled the capitalist institutions to go on working in ,spite of the loss of markets, and provided resources out of which the unemployed could be maintained at a standard of life just high enough not to drive them to mass despair. There were, accordingly, in Great Britain, neither the conditions requisite for the rise of a strong fascist movement, nor the need for such a movement as an instrument for the preservation of capitalism. There is, therefore, no powerful fascist organisation in Great Britain— yet. There soon would be, if the conditions called for it, and if British socialism were not strong enough to crush it by prompt measures before it had been able to take effective hold.

4 IMPLICATIONS OF THE WAR

We have, then, in Europe today, three systems working side by side, and one not yet working anywhere, but trying to challenge all three. Now all these three systems under the existing conditions of insecurity have been compelled to divert a large part of their productive energies into production for war. This applies, or has applied up to the past few months, least to Great Britain, both because Great Britain was late in starting, and because of the magnitude of the resources lying ready to be used. But of course it applies almost equally to Great Britain and to Germany today. This diversion of resources to war production of itself imposes a certain similarity on all countries which resort to it; for under any system it involves a high degree of centralised control and an approach to totalitarian method of government and organisation. This process has indeed gone less far in Great Britain than elsewhere, though we complain of it. France is, today, much more totalitarian than Great Britain in its methods of wartime control.

Now wartime totalitarianism, whatever its economic basis, whether it be capitalist, or fascist, or communist, necessarily presents certain features which are at least in form socialistic, and has, at any rate temporarily, certain equalising effects on social classes. The consciousness of this was doubtless one reason for Mr. Chamberlain's eagerness to pursue the policy of appeasement; and he and those who think with him stand in great fear of war as a destroyer of the relatively free and liberal capitalism of the English tradition. This fear of destroying liberal capitalism combined with their fear of communism to make them wish to avoid war with Germany by every possible means, and, if war must come, to divert it at the earliest possible moment into a struggle against the Soviet Union.

Totalitarianism, already pushed in Germany almost to the limit, has necessarily meant a great deal of assimilation of the Nazi system to Russian methods of centralised control. It has also, on the home front, necessarily strengthened the left wing of Nazism, which sees in the useless consumption of the rich a waste of national resources needed either for the increase of military strength or for the maintenance of the people at a minimum standard compatible

I

with national efficiency. Accordingly, we find Germany moving further and further away from the traditions of free capitalism under the stress of war, and advancing towards a position that may require a sort of compulsory 'socialism' as the result of the complete exhaustion of any surplus wealth available for consumption by the rich. This does not mean in the very least that the leaders of Nazism are socialists in desire or intention. They are, in fact, at bottom, neither socialists nor capitalists, but lunatic gangsters imbued with a doctrine of militarist nationalism and an unqualified belief in the virtues of sheer force.

Capitalism, in this war, is represented not by fascism, which is compelled to squeeze the capitalists in the interests of military power, but by *us*. The working classes in Great Britain have failed even seriously to shake the authority of British capitalism : the British Empire still sprawls across the globe. Why should we expect Stalin to love us—save for the one reason that we are fighting Hitler, who has hitherto been his most formidable enemy? We cannot get away from the fact that, from the standpoint of the 20th century, Great Britain stands for an obsolete, rentier, imperialistic capitalism, essentially uncreative and obstructive. We cannot get away from the fact that this British capitalism has shown itself ready to compromise with fascism up to the very last moment, or that it has maintained a consistent hostility to the Soviet Union, even while it was negotiating with it in the name of collective security. Whatever institutions may fit the needs of the 20th century, assuredly those of British or of French capitalism do not fit these needs. They are sufficiently condemned by their endemic unemployment, and by their failure, despite the vast opportunities which science has opened up to our generation, to create anything at all.

To say this is not to deny that British and French capitalism possesses certain highly significant virtues. Under their economic sway there have grown up certain habits of living and certain cultural traditions which are of the very greatest value. They have meant something real, albeit limited, in terms of human freedom and of social culture. But the possession of these virtues cannot alter the fact that economically our capitalism is out of date, and cannot ever be made again to bear the fruits of human progress. If we are determined to preserve the cultural and social gains of the 19th century, we must find means of establishing new economic institutions capable of safeguarding them under the changed conditions of the 20th century world.

It would surely be intolerable, to any decent-minded or sensible person, to fight this war for the purpose of re-establishing the supremacy of this uncreative capitalism, of restoring it to power in Germany on the ruins of Nazi domination, and of building up a new League of Limpets against the Soviet Union. I find it impossible to blame Stalin for seeing the war in this light; for this is precisely how our own Government would wish to regard it—in full agreement with many supporters of the League of Nations and with many new-style Federal Unionists of the right wing. They are out to make war, not in order that men

may be free to build up a new world adapted to the
conditions of the 20th century, but in order to restore
the *status quo ante* Hitler, with a *cordon sanitaire*
round the territories of the Soviet Union. I can see
why Stalin thinks he had better help the Nazis to stop
that, especially as the strain of war upon the Nazi
system, added to the endeavours of the enemies of
Germany to persuade the Germans into a revolution
of the correct capitalist sort, may actually have the
effect of driving Germany to the left, towards communism as the only alternative. For fascism is no abiding
place: it is a war system which must go either to the
right, towards naked oppression, or to the left, against
capitalism, if it is to survive at all. I can see Stalin
saying to himself: Why should not I, why should
not the Soviet Union, profit by the contradictions in
which Nazism and western capitalism are alike
involved?

This logic would be valid under the conditions of
today if the impotence of democratic socialism could
be assumed. If there are, in truth, only three practical
alternatives for the world of today—a capitalism which
can be bolstered up for a time but never again endowed
with any creative force, a fascism which is self-
destructive because its very philosophy compels it
to tear the world to pieces by war, and a communism
which at any rate holds out the promise that some
day the dictatorship of the proletariat will give way
to the full freedom of the cooperative commonwealth—
then there is no question which of the three ought to
be preferred. If I do not accept Stalin's answer, it
is because I am not prepared to write off democratic

socialism, despite all its failures and vacillations of recent years, as a total loss. I believe that the democratic socialist solution is practicable, and is the one means whereby we can hope to build the cooperative commonwealth without destroying those values of tolerance and culture which have been able to grow up inside capitalism and gradually to extend their influence in the advanced capitalist countries over an increasing proportion of the people. Democratic socialism offers the only means of building the new order upon what is valuable and worth preserving in the civilisation of today—instead of beginning with the destruction of all these values, and thereafter, to the accompaniment of an enormous amount of avoidable human suffering, having to build them up again from the very foundations. Because I believe this, I believe that it is worth while to fight against fascist aggression. But it is only worth while to fight Hitler if we are fighting for socialism—democratic socialism—and not for Mr. Chamberlain and the restoration of the obsolete institutions in which he still believes. On this basis, I support the war; but is this the basis on which the British Labour movement is giving its support? Is this the direction in which the Labour Party is trying to lead the people?

I want to know, not merely what settlement the Labour Party proposes for the affairs of Europe, but also what are its war aims in Great Britain—on the home front. Unless British socialists mean to make socialism in Great Britain the basis for the peace, the war is not worth fighting, and the idea of victory in it is meaningless from a socialist point of view. Unless this is the war aim for which we mean to fight, I say emphatically that I do not want victory, either for Germany, or for a Britain still led by Mr. Chamberlain into the slough of despond. I prefer stalemate to a Chamberlain victory. But I continue to hope, despite all the appearances to the contrary, that British socialism may yet assert itself with a policy, a propaganda, and an agitation that will make this war worth while, because it will make plain that the war aim of British Labour is nothing less than the establishment of democratic socialism in Great Britain, and the promotion of a democratic socialist revolution throughout capitalist Europe as the basis for a constructive peace.

6

WAR AND PREPARATIONS
FOR PEACE

K. ZILLIACUS

WAR AND PREPARATIONS FOR PEACE

NOTE.—I had better begin this essay with a word of personal explanation. I undertook to write it many months ago and prepared most of it before the outbreak of the present war. Since its preparation I have taken up war work of an official character. But I remain a Labour Candidate and retain my political rights as such, although I exercise them within the limits imposed by wartime conditions. I therefore wish to emphasise first that this essay will not contain any information not available to the public—that will be sufficiently obvious as it proceeds. Second, that no one is responsible for any views I express but myself.

1 THE MEANING OF REAL PEACE

THE task before us is to analyse the present situation and to draw from this analysis certain conclusions as to what we ought to do if we want real peace.

My definition of real peace is a settlement that will lay the foundations of a society in which the values of civilisation can flourish. That means a society in which the State exists for man and not man for the State, in which we are constantly striving to realise the principles that men should have the right to choose their rulers; to enjoy free speech and association; to live under the rule of law, that is the right to trial by an independent judiciary, and freedom from arbitrary interference by the executive authority; the right to work and the right to free education, the right to a minimum standard of living and to free care of the aged and the sick and those incapable of working. In fact, a democratic society based not only on the old personal rights of man proclaimed by the French Revolution but also on the 20th century social and economic rights which the Russian Revolution set out to achieve. In our complex, highly organised world it is only in such a society that the arts and sciences can flourish and man can attain his full stature.

The world today is a hideous contradiction of almost all we believe essential to the good life. Tyranny, mendacity, hate and fear are rampant, and the energies of the civilised world are concentrated on war and preparations for war. This nightmare has gone on and got worse ever since 1931. Today, war in peace-time has culminated in a sort of peace in war-time, and the latter is moving to some monstrous climax.

Our minds are stunned by the march of awful events, and our capacity for emotion is exhausted by what the world has suffered in a crescendo of horrors during the last few years.

The one unforgivable sin in this situation is fatalism and apathy. Whether we wish it or not we are actors, not spectators, in this drama. Our job is to know what we want. The Chinese philosopher and revolu-tionary leader, Dr. Sun Yat Sen, had a favourite aphorism 'To know is hard, to act is easy.' That sounds like a paradox—how can it be harder to know what one wants than to get it after one does know? The truth of the aphorism lies in the amount of significance packed into the phrase 'know what you want.'

To know what one wants means first to understand what is happening; second to be clear in our own minds as to the end we desire; and third to will the means as well as the end. These three things are interdependent, and the most difficult and important is the third.

I propose to deliver this lecture under these three headings.

2 THE PRESENT SITUATION

First, therefore, let us try to understand what is happening. Why are we at war? Why has democracy disappeared over a large part of Europe and got into difficulties elsewhere? Why has fascism become a major menace to peace and civilisation? What is the malady that is afflicting our disordered and distraught world? Why has the Great War to end war and to make the world safe for democracy ended in this? Why did the great adventure of the League of Nations, the attempt to organise the world for peace, fail so lamentably?

The answer to that last question will give us the clue we seek to read the riddle of our present discontents. For the drift to war is the obverse of the failure to organise the world for peace. The explanation of the reasons for the latter is the analysis of the causes of the former.

I therefore make no apology for devoting considerable time to the question of why the League has failed, since it has a direct bearing on the present

situation and on the political conclusions we ought
to draw from it.

And in speaking on this subject I am, as a Spanish
saying has it, 'speaking out of the mouth of my
wound,' for I was for nineteen years an official of the
League of Nations Secretariat and have lived through
the whole story of the League from start to finish.
There is nothing like protracted failure in spite of all
we can do to avert it to make people think. The
shattering blows that destroyed the collective system
piecemeal between 1931 and 1938 certainly made us
League officials think. My own thought began with
blaming individual statesmen for what they did or
failed to do at Geneva. It then became clear that they
were acting on the instructions of their governments.
Investigation and reflection on the decisions of governments made it clear that their action or inaction was
determined by sincerely held views about what was
best in the national interest, and that these views were
shaped by social and economic factors that influenced
the sub-conscious minds of our rulers even more than
their conscious decisions.

I will not take you through the mental process by
which I was very reluctantly compelled, by hard facts,
to arrive at the views I hold at present. But I will
pick out for you one or two facts about the League
which I think point quite clearly to the correct
conclusion as to the reasons for its failure.

For one thing, it is now generally recognised that
the League failed because the Covenant did not go
far enough in subordinating national sovereignty to
some form of international authority and in particular

did not bind the member states to cooperate in economic matters. But why did the Covenant fail to do these things? Not because nobody put forward these ideas, for they were in fact propounded, but because they were successfully resisted. Resisted by whom? By international toryism and plutocracy, that is, by the Right in politics. What was the motive that compelled the Right to adopt this attitude of clinging to national sovereignty and economic anarchy?

The origin and fate of the proposals for economic cooperation at the Peace Conference give the plainest possible answer to this question. An article in the *New Statesman and Nation* in 1917, attributed to the pen of Mr. Sidney Webb, first launched the idea that the wartime economic and financial controls, covering raw materials, shipping and transport, loans, etc., should at the Armistice be internationalised by the addition of neutrals and ex-enemies, put under the League and used for peacetime reconstruction purposes. This idea was taken up first by the British Labour Party and Trade Union Congress and later by the whole inter-allied labour and socialist movement. It was urged so strongly that the British Government put forward proposals at the Peace Conference going some way in this direction.

Professor Zimmern, in his book *The League of Nations and the Rule of Law* (pp. 114–115) says that if these proposals had been accepted by the Governments 'the new states, such as Germany, would have started on their careers under very different economic and psychological conditions from those which they had actually to face . . . this would have had a powerful influence on the whole subsequent development.' The League would have been built on firm economic foundations and the peoples would have had before their eyes

> from the moment of the firing of the last gun of the war an example of international cooperation for peaceful and beneficent purposes, touching them closely in their rights and activities. In such an atmosphere, with such a working model before their eyes, the elaboration of the political machinery and functions of the League of Nations would no longer have seemed a visionary enterprise provoking doubt and scepticism in practical minds. . . . If the peace, as is so often said, was lost, its first great defeat, perhaps its greatest defeat of all, was suffered not in the Peace Conference itself, but during the days and weeks immediately following the Armistice, when the economic forces were allowed to slip out of the control of statesmanship.

Why was it that this excellent scheme that was strongly backed by the international Labour and Socialist movement was rejected at the Peace Conference? Chiefly at the instigation of Mr. Herbert Hoover, the U S Minister of Commerce. Mr. Hoover was a big business man and his representative at Paris, Mr. Bernard Baruch, was a big American financier. He rejected the scheme in a letter to Lord Cecil of 12 April 1919, which contains as its key sentence 'The salvation of the world must rest upon the initiative of individuals.'

Mr. Hoover and Mr. Baruch were acting in this matter not as individuals but as typical representatives of big business, not only in the United States but also in France and Great Britain. The moment the war drew to a close there was tremendous pressure by plutocracy in these countries to scrap the wartime controls and restrictions on private profit-making. This was the force that controlled the Governments and defeated the demands of the workers.

The origin and fate of the proposals for economic cooperation were only one reflection of the clash at the Peace Conference between the rival forces of plutocracy and the working class, in which plutocracy won most of the time, though it had to compromise on some points. There were, in fact, three camps in the Allied countries at the end of the war. On the Right were plutocracy and toryism. Their programme was the 'knock-out blow'—that is a military victory and a dictated peace based on the imperialist and annexationist secret treaties, plus a war of intervention against the Russian revolution and any attempt at social revolution in Europe.

On the Left were the revolutionary elements in the working class who believed that only through replacing capitalism by socialism could the foundations of a permanent peace be laid. This they further believed could not be accomplished except by revolution, leading through a period of so-called proletarian dictatorship to complete social and political democracy, within the framework of a World Union of Socialist Republics.

In the middle were moderates, liberal, labour and progressive opinion, large in numbers but less clear cut in their views than either of the extremes. This middle-of-the-road opinion, whose prophet was Wilson, agreed with the revolutionary Left that the war showed the need for rebuilding the foundations of civilisation on the basis of world government, democracy and social justice. But they shared the horror of the Right for revolution, and believed that what they wanted could better be achieved by gradual and piecemeal methods.

The result of the clash between these three camps at the Peace Conference and of the social forces behind them was that the Wilsonian progressives compromised with plutocracy and toryism on the basis of a very weak League and a bad peace settlement rather than find themselves giving support to the revolutionary Left as the result of a break with the Tories.

Two quotations will illustrate clearly how this process worked, and I think cast a bright light on the reasons for the failure of the vast body of well-meaning Lib-Lab, middle-of-the-road progressives to make their will prevail in the post-war world.

The first quotation is from the minutes of a statement by President Wilson to the American Delegation on his way to the Peace Conference on board the ss. *George Washington*. Wilson's remarks were taken down at the time by one of the delegates and read as follows:

The President remarked that we would be the only disinterested people at the Peace Conference, and that *the men whom we were about to deal with did not represent their own peoples.* . . . With great earnestness he re-emphasised the point that unless the conference was prepared to follow the opinions of mankind and to express the will of the people rather than that of their leaders at the conference, we should soon be involved in *another break-up* of the world, and when such a break-up came it would not be a war but a cataclysm.

A few months later, on 3 March, 1919, we find Colonel House, Wilson's most intimate collaborator, writing in melancholy vein in his diary:

> It is now evident that the peace will not be such a peace as I had hoped, or one which this terrible upheaval should have brought about. . . . If the President should exert his influence among the liberals and labouring classes, he might possibly overthrow the Governments in Great Britain, France and Italy; but if he did he would still have to reckon with our people; and he might bring the whole world into chaos. The overthrow of Governments might not end there, and it would be a grave responsibility for any man to take at this time.

So that you see in December, Wilson said that unless the Conference expressed the will of the peoples rather than that of the Governments that failed to represent them 'we should soon be involved in another break-up of the world, and when such a war came it would not be a war but a cataclysm.' And in March we find Colonel House recording that Wilson, when faced by the choice between telling the peoples who trusted him the truth about the kind of peace their Governments were making and accepting the bad peace they had made, thereby betraying the peoples, preferred the latter alternative. And he preferred it not because he believed that the peoples would not listen if he told them the truth, but, on the contrary, precisely because he was afraid they would take him at his word and proceed to overthrow the Governments that had betrayed peace and civilisation.

Revolution seemed a greater evil than unrighteousness, although it is only fair to add that the latter

K

was tempered by hope. Wilson and his followers consoled themselves for the badness of the Versailles Treaty and the weakness of the League by vastly exaggerating the potential capacity of the latter to grow strong and to redeem their failures at some unspecified future date.

I suggest that the historic error of liberalism and social democracy in the years since the last war is illustrated by the above quotations, and is exemplified again and again in the history of those years. This has been to prefer in the last analysis capitulation to reaction to cooperation with revolutionaries. I say this not as a revolutionary but as a democrat, as the kind of socialist who believes that socialism is the heir to liberalism and will fulfil the promise of liberalism. I am not a social pacifist any more than I am an international pacifist, but also I am not a revolutionary any more than I am a militarist. I regard both war and revolution as great evils, which must be avoided at almost any cost, but which may sometimes be a lesser evil than surrender. Where we have democracy it would not only be folly but criminal not to use it, and to defend it to the utmost—but we can do that more effectively if we realise the danger that some, at least, of the other side may be tempted to change the rules when they fear they may lose the game.

Whether one studies the history of the Russian revolution or of the Italian and German counter-revolutions the same pattern emerges. The Mensheviks and social revolutionaries in Russia endeavoured to cooperate with progressive capitalist parties in a middle-of-the-road policy, whose avowed purpose was to defend political democracy against the attempts of the Bolsheviks on the Left to carry out a social revolution, and the Tsarist counter-revolution on the Right. That policy ended in their sinking into complete futility or else being dragged in the wake of their capitalist partners most of the way into the camp of the Tsarist generals and of the advocates of intervention.

The German Social Democrats adopted precisely the same policy, and as a result began by calling in the Prussian generals to shoot down the revolutionary workers, and ended by capitulating to Hitler. All these things were done in the name of democracy and consistently avoiding violence and bloodshed.

The fact that we can now in retrospect indulge in wisdom after the event and understand why the progressives failed does not, of course, mean that we are entitled to condemn them or to underestimate their difficulties. The Revolutionary Left and the Soviet Union in those days, as now, were, to say the least of it, exceedingly difficult to work with on any terms except those of surrender to all their demands and unqualified acceptance of their leadership. Nevertheless, the fact of failure is so plain and its consequences so portentous that we ought to be able to draw the correct political conclusion and apply it to the circumstances of today.

The League experiment flourished modestly in the short period between the first post-war slump and the great slump, when it looked as though the pre-war economic system was going to be restored and was going to work. The great slump put an end to those hopes. It made it clear that the economic system was in need of far-reaching reconstruction if it were to afford the minimum of satisfaction necessary to prevent an embittered struggle between the Haves and the Have-nots on the social front.

The partial breakdown of capitalism in the great slump was largely due to the increasing concentration of economic and financial power in great trusts and combines, giant banks, etc., and the misuse of their powers by the plutocracy at the expense of the rest of the community. The further development of large scale monopoly capitalism and the pressure of pluto-cracy in the direction of economic nationalism, war preparations and political reaction, are all phenomena directly traceable to the great slump, although their roots lie far back in the past. Viewed in the light of its social origins and purposes, fascism is a form of capitalist counter-revolution. The very structure of fascist states compels them to policies of expansion and aggression when they cannot satisfy the social needs to which they appealed in order to get into power and must therefore provide their peoples with blood and circuses.

The retreat of the pluto-democracies and the advance of fascism, the collapse of the collective system and the return of the world to the jungle of power-politics are principally due to the struggle of the possessing classes to hold on to their power and profits in spite of the conditions created by the slump. The sated imperialisms of France and Great Britain were in a dilemma when faced by the hungry and barbaric imperialisms of fascism : they were as much afraid of the revolutionary consequences of successful collective resistance to fascist aggression as they were of war ensuing from the failure to organise collective resistance. In fact, they chose the latter alternative, partly out of intense desire for peace at almost any price, but partly, too, for less creditable class motives.

But sooner or later this process was bound to end in the fascist States over-reaching themselves and pressing France and Great Britain so hard that the latter felt compelled to risk war rather than yield again. When this did happen it took place in almost the worst conceivable circumstances. After having let down democratic Spain and Czechoslovakia when the odds were heavily in our favour and we had the Soviet Union on our side for the asking, we finally blundered into war for the semi-fascist Polish State, whose foreign policy bore an unenviable responsibility for its own troubles, after the Soviet Union had concluded a treaty of friendship and non-aggression with Nazi Germany.

There is a good deal to be said for the view of the extreme Left that the world is in a colossal mess, a clash of rival imperialisms, a civil war within capitalism which continues the contradictions of capitalism by different means. I do not think this view exhausts the question, because I believe there is a real difference between even capitalist democracy and fascism, but I admit there is a good deal in it, and I think it is useful to realise that fact as the antidote to the complacent and too simple view generally taken of this conflict.

3 WHAT OUGHT TO BE DONE?

In this situation it is incumbent upon us to think out what ought to be done in order that this war shall end on terms compatible with the survival of the democratic values. There are three possible courses which we should examine:

1. The first is the demand for an immediate Peace Conference. Those who hold this view are in a small minority. I disagree completely with this demand. But for that very reason I feel we ought to consider it fully and fairly so as to understand precisely why it is not acceptable. Those who advocate this view do so partly on the assumption that it really would be possible to convert the Government to it and partly on the opposite assumption that advocating this policy would be a way of rallying the forces of the Left against the Government. Let us consider each assumption in turn.

As regards the former, it is believed that if the Government could be induced to enter a conference today with Germany and Italy and the Soviet Union and possibly the United States as well as an assortment of smaller powers (and, of course, France) the result would be a situation which would give the Soviet Union and the forces of the Left in France and Great Britain a chance to prevail against the fascist regimes and the reactionary British and French Governments. I believe that this view is the exact opposite of the truth: those who were 'appeasers' in France and Great Britain were converted to the necessity for defending their empires only very reluctantly and at the last moment. They continue to be acutely aware of the dilemma that a victory against Hitler will almost certainly be a defeat for capitalism. This or that individual statesman may now be convinced beyond the possibility of change of the necessity for fighting to the end. But the forces which have thrown up these statesmen are quite capable of reverting to appeasement as soon as they are convinced that public opinion will tolerate such a policy. If, therefore, the campaign of the communists, fascists and pacifists (surely an oddly assorted combination!) were to succeed and France and Great Britain were to enter a Peace Conference with Hitler unconditionally it would mean that they had decided to recognise Hitler as the conqueror of Central Europe (most of Poland and the whole of Czechoslovakia) and to bargain with him on this basis. They could only do so if they were prepared to make colonial concessions as well. The only motive powerful enough to justify such a course would be the desire of reaction and plutocracy in France and Great Britain to get together with the fascist regimes against their common enemy—the working class not only in the West but throughout Europe.

Nor do I believe that we can safely trust the Soviet Union to save us from the consequences of compounding with reaction and fascism. If there is one thing clear about the Soviet Union's foreign policy today it is that they are concerned exclusively with the extension of their own territory and influence by the methods of power-politics, and have abandoned any idea of solidarity with the proletariat of other

countries. No doubt in the minds of the rulers of
Soviet Russia they are indirectly serving the international interests of the working class by looking after
their own national interests, for they assume that there
can never be any conflict between the two. But
that does not alter the fact that the USSR are committed to recognising Hitler's claim to tyrannise over
the Poles and the Czechs, and indeed to regarding
Hitler as a lesser evil than the British and French
Governments. That being the position, we cannot
expect much help from the Soviet Union.

The small powers would be a cipher at a conference.
Italy would be on the side of Germany; the United
States would not take an active part, and would be in
favour of patching up some kind of deal on any terms
whatever between the two sides.

The result of such a conference would be to rivet
the hold of reaction and fascism on Europe and to
revert in an aggravated form to the state of war in
peacetime that ended in the present war, and would
end once more in a major conflict.

The second assumption of those advocating an
immediate Peace Conference is that the Government
would resist the proposal under all circumstances and
that it would therefore serve as a rallying cry to all
who wish to end the war by revolution. Those who
take this line are fond of pointing to the example of
Lenin and the Bolsheviks in Russia. But they should
be consistent. Lenin argued frankly that the defeat
of Tsarist Russia by Germany was a lesser evil than
the continuation of the imperialist war. He supported
this argument by pointing out that Russian Tsarism

was the most reactionary of all the. belligerent Governments.

Those who want a revolution in this country must therefore will the means as well as the end and admit frankly that they consider that British toryism is a greater evil than German fascism and that therefore they prefer the defeat of this country by Hitler to continuing the war. That, in fact, is almost the position being adopted today by a good many communists and pacifists—not to mention Sir Oswald Mosley's little lot. I can only say that I passionately disagree with it. Say what you like about toryism and plutocracy in this country, and I have said a lot in the past and intend to say much more in the future, but there is, nevertheless, an enormous difference in civilisation between what we have and the conditions in Germany. Democracy can correct its mistakes; it can change and evolve into something better. Whereas fascism cannot—it is irredeemably bad, and will only get worse, until it is broken up by defeat and revolution and something else takes its place.

2. The second possible alternative is one already being advocated by some of the extreme Right here, but more particularly in France, namely, a military victory and a dictated peace. The experience of the last war showed that no power can be trusted with dictatorial powers over a beaten foe. The political consequences of the last dictated peace should be sufficient to warn us against repeating the experiment. In any case there will be very serious military difficulties. Captain Liddell-Hart in the *Defence of Britain* drew attention to the fact that owing to the superiority

of the defence over the offence, the enormous resources mobilised on both sides, the shortness of the front and the depth of the fortified zone, the holes in the blockade owing to the number of neutrals and the partial cooperation of the Soviet Union with Germany, it would be exceedingly difficult and a matter of years to reach a point at which one side would really be decisively defeated. He argues powerfully for the view that we must not strain after victory in this sense but limit our objective to making the enemy give up hope of victory. When this happens there will be an upheaval in Germany and a real chance of a negotiated peace on decent terms.

3. Captain Liddell-Hart, in effect, is in favour of the third alternative, which is also that of the Labour Party, namely, to go on fighting until there is a revolution in Germany and then to negotiate an agreed peace with a revolutionary Germany. This peace should be on the following principles: a. The setting up of some form of international authority on as wide a foundation as possible in which sovereignty and defence should be pooled to a much higher degree than under the Geneva Covenant and in which economic cooperation should go much farther. A policy of colonial emancipation under international control should also be part and parcel of the foundations of the new international organisation. b. Within the framework of this organisation the Poles and Czechs and other oppressed nationalities should be enabled to enjoy complete national autonomy within ethnographical limits.

This view of the kind of peace settlement to strive

for is based on the belief that the attempt at the last
Peace Conference to set up some form of world government resting on democracy and world justice must be
resumed, but on lines that profit by the errors of
the past and take account of the realities of the
present. Those who believe in this policy must will
the means as well as the end.

4 THE MEANS TO THE END

It is clear that no such reconstruction of Europe can
be attempted so long as the Nazi regime remains in
Germany and maintains its occupation of Poland
and Czechoslovakia and its influence over a large part
of Central Europe and the Balkans, where it is bolstering
up semi-fascist regimes. It is, however, clear that if
and when the Nazi regime is overthrown by the
German people Nazi rule and influence will collapse
over a large part of Central and South-Eastern Europe
and be followed by revolutionary movements which
are likely to go all the way to social revolution. In
one way or another the USSR, which is now a Central
European Power, and the communist parties and
their adherents are likely to be mixed up with these
revolutionary movements.

On the other hand the course that is being advocated
in various reactionary quarters in this country and
France might end easily in the two Governments
supporting Prussian generals, 'moderate' Nazis, the
Habsburgs, the Wittelsbachs and even the Hohen-
zollerns, and attempting to deal with the situation
resulting from the overthrow of the Nazis by backing
pure reaction. The support of Italy in the Balkans is

another possible outcome of this policy. That may be a simplification of what is bound to be an exceedingly confused situation. The development of Soviet foreign policy, for instance, may bring that country further and further into the Nazi camp and finally draw her into the war on the wrong side. Hitler is also playing on an international scale the same game of social demagogy by which the Nazis came into power. That is, he is telling the German workers that Nazi Germany, with the support and sympathy of the USSR, is fighting western plutocracy and imperialism in the interests of the German masses. The net result may be some kind of Bolshevisation from above of Nazi Germany, which while ultimately leading to revolution would, for a time, strengthen her unity with the USSR.

In this situation those who want the kind of peace settlement I have outlined must, I think, draw one negative and one positive conclusion: the negative conclusion is that under no circumstances and on no pretext must we be drawn into or support a war of intervention against revolutions on the Continent. If intervention does begin it will be on the pretext of supporting continental social democrats and middle-of-the-road progressives in the name of defending democracy against the rival extremes of revolution and counter-revolution, just as happened over intervention in Russia. There are plenty of Kerenskys and Casados in the Europe of today ready to play their pitiful and foolish parts. Instead of letting themselves be led up the interventionist garden, the forces of the Left in general, and Labour in particular, must be ready to oppose any attempt at the end of this war to back European counter-revolution with the same energy as they opposed intervention in Russia in 1920.

The positive conclusion is that the sooner it becomes possible to negotiate with the Soviet Union the better. We cannot achieve any settlement of Central Europe without negotiating with the USSR as well as with a revolutionary Germany. If the Soviet Union were to come into the war on the side of Germany it would be impossible, so huge would be the forces on both sides, to end the war in any way except by a negotiated peace.

The development of Soviet foreign policy since August, and particularly the war of aggression on Finland and the prospect of resort to similar tactics in the Balkans, make it exceedingly difficult even to advocate negotiations with the Soviet Union. Nevertheless, the best way of saving Finland from the complete destruction of her independence would be for France and Great Britain to offer mediation on the basis of readiness to conclude a Non-Aggression Treaty with the Soviet Union and to settle all outstanding issues with her and to give any guarantees in reason the Russians can ask against our joining in a capitalist coalition against them, in return for the Soviet Government satisfying her main strategic demands in Finland without destroying the independence of that country.

Similarly, Soviet pressure on Rumania or other Balkan States would be a situation that could be met only by agreement between the USSR and the

Western Powers. In fact, in almost every conceivable situation, including that of the Soviet Union joining in the war on the side of Germany, an attempt at settlement by negotiation would still be the best policy. For that reason it should be urged and continually urged by the Left in this country.

There remains the problem of France. French reaction is in the saddle, and is mercilessly exploiting the workers. At the same time the two countries are being forced by the necessities of the war to effect a partial fusion of their defence forces and economic systems as well as to remain in constant touch politically. The Left, and particularly Labour, in this country, it will be hoped, will not repeat the mistake made at the end of the last war, namely, of confusing French reaction with the French people and of having no positive answer to the French demand for security.

What French reaction means by security is the break-up of Germany and the restoration of the Holy Roman Empire. To that demand there is bound to be unalterable opposition, not only by the Left but by the majority of British opinion. But what inducement are we to offer to the French people to dissociate themselves from this particular way of achieving security?

The most hopeful method, it may be suggested, would be for Labour to offer, in return for the French Government accepting Labour's principles of a peace settlement, including Labour's colonial policy, to support the immediate conclusion of a treaty with France which would enlarge and put on a permanent basis and provide for the conversion to peacetime

purposes of all the economic, military and political
cooperation that already exists between the two
countries. We should, in fact, favour the setting up of
a semi-Federal Union between France and Great
Britain as a nucleus for the European Federation to
be set up at the Peace Conference by negotiation with
a revolutionary Germany and Central Europe and with,
as far as possible, the Soviet Union.

If Labour and the Left generally would advocate
some such policy now, which would include the
pledging of both countries to a Charter of the democratic Rights of Man, the effect would be very considerable on public opinion not only in this country
but also in France and the USA. We should, for the
first time, have a sort of working model of the kind
of world that we wish to build, and we should make
it clear to the German people that they could join in
this Union on equal terms the moment they overthrew
their rulers and evacuated Poland and Czechoslovakia.[1]

Well, I have analysed as clearly as I can the situation
today as I see it, and have drawn the conclusion that
we must, in conjunction with France, continue the
war until there is a revolution in Germany, and that
we must then cooperate with a revolutionary Central
Europe, and so far as we possibly can, with the Soviet

[1] Cf. the following report in the *Sunday Times* of 31 December
of M. Daladier's speech on 29 December: 'The greatest interest
has been aroused here by a passage in M. Daladier's speech before
the Senate last night, in which the Premier suggested that federal
links might be established between the British and French Empires;
that the present Anglo-French economic, financial and military
cooperation was only a beginning; and that the 'federal' system,
if inaugurated, might be opened to other States. M. Daladier
thought that the Anglo-French agreement might serve as the
nucleus for the future Federation of Europe.'

Union, in laying the foundations of a new social and international order in Europe.

I should be less frank than I feel it my duty to be if I did not say at this point that I do not believe any such policy as that I have suggested will be pursued until we have a government in which Labour is playing a big part, and from which those chiefly responsible for the disastrous policy of appeasement, which has brought us to the present pass, are removed.

These are dark and difficult times, and what is needed above all are courage and faith—courage to see facts as they are, however unpleasant they may be, and to will the means realistically that are necessary to achieve our end, and faith in choosing and cleaving to a worthy end—nothing less than the final abolition of war through the uniting of humanity in some form of World Union or World Federation, resting on social justice, democracy and racial equality.

THE END